Situational English

Kim Seon-Ock

SUN MOON UNIVERSITY

책머리에

저자가 대학에서 영어를 가르쳐온 이래 언제나 떨쳐버릴 수 없었던 아쉬움이 있었는데, 그것은 실제대화에 활용 가능한 내용의 회화영어를 익히는 데에 적합한 교재를 집필하는 것이었다. 영어회화 시간에 사용하는 거의 대부분의 교재가 중·고등학교 때부터 해 왔던 인사말부터 시작하기 때문에 학생들이 실생활에 적용할 수 있는 상황중심영어표현을 배울 기회가 없다는 점이 늘 안타까웠다. 회화 교재임에도 불구하고 문법 중심의 단원을 공부하다보면 학생들은 회화를 하기 보다는 문법을 배우는 시간이 되는 경우가 많다. 이에 표현중심의 영어회화 교재의 필요성을 절실히 느낀 저자가 오늘에야 비로소 실용영어를 구사할 수 있는 교재를 펴내게 되었다.

본 교재는 일반 영어학습자들의 회화 학습교재로도 사용할 수 있으며 대학의 한 학기 실용영어회화 교재로도 사용할 수 있도록 총 15개 단원으로 구성하였다. 매 단원은 CONVERSATION을 통해 간단한 상황중심 대화를 익히고 나면 VOCABULARY를 통해 그 단원과 관련된 영어 어휘를 공부하고, 그와 관련된 표현들을 KEY EXPRESSIONS & APPLICATION DIALOGUES에서 보충할 수 있게 하였으며, REVIEW에서 영작 문제를 제시하여 매 단원에서 배운 유용한 상황 표현들을 확실히 기억할 수 있도록 복습의 기회를 제공하고 있다. 그리고 기타 유용한 영어의 관용어 표현과 더불어 영어회화의 기본 어휘와 표현들을 부록으로 정리하여 필요하면 보충자료로 충분히 활용할 수 있도록 하였다.

대화의 구성과 핵심 표현들은 실생활에서 자주 쓰는 상황별 영어 표현들을 활용하였으므로 학습자들이 긴요한 표현들을 하나씩 외워가다 보면 어떤 상황에 부닥쳤을 때 요긴하게 활용할 수 있을 것이다. 다만 지면의 제약으로 인하여, 그간에 준비했던 많은 자료들을 제대로 망라하지 못했음을 밝혀두는 바이다.

원래 외국어를 배울 때에는 자주 쓰는 말부터 익혀야하는데, 실제 교육현장에서는 회화에 필요한 구어표현(colloquial expressions)보다는 문법적인 수준에 근거하여 회화를 할 때에 자연스러운 흐름보다는 문법에 맞추는 식의 어색한 회화교육이 실시되고 있는 것이 현실이다. 그렇기 때문에 실제 상황에서 하고 싶은 말이 있어도 꿀 먹은 벙어리가 되기 마련이다. 상황별 영어회화 표현을 많이 익히면서 영어 원어민과 회화를 병행한다면 훨씬 더 효율적인 영어 학습이 될 것임을 확신한다. 반드시 학생들에게 도움이 되는 책을 써야겠다는 다짐을 하면서 노심초사를 거듭하였으나 원래 의도한 바에 미치지 못한 것 같은 아쉬움이 남는다.

이 책이 세상에 햇빛을 볼 수 있도록 끊임없는 격려와 더불어 저술방향의 지남(指南)이 되어주신 단국대학교 영어과 김문수 박사님께 감사드린다. 아울러 국제화시대 외국어교육의 요람으로 올바른 학문의 길을 베푸는 선문대학교에 감사한다. 더욱이 이 책이 나오기까지 온갖 정성을 다하신 선문대학교 출판부 관계자 여러분에게 감사의 뜻을 전하고 싶다. 마지막으로, 이 세상 끝까지 저자에게 힘이 되어주는 가족들에게 머리 숙여 감사드린다.

이제 용기를 내어 이 책을 내어놓으면서 저자는 앞으로 이 책을 강의에 활용함으로써 교육효과를 극대화할 수 있는 방향으로 가필과 정정을 계속하겠다는 겸허한 약속으로 머리말을 맺는 바이다.

2008년 11월

저자 김 선 옥(金 仙 玉)

Contents

시추에이셔널 잉글리쉬

Situational English

Unit 00 *Situational English*

일상생활 관련표현

01 Conversation

[I watch some ABC News, first thing in the morning!]

Min-ho : What's the first thing you do in the morning, Emily?

Emily : Well, I go to the bathroom and take a shower.
And then I eat some cereal with milk for breakfast.
How about you?

Min-ho : I turn on the computer and **watch some ABC News, first thing in the morning.** And then I have breakfast, brush my teeth, wash my face, and wear some toner and perfume.

Emily : What time do you leave home for school?

Min-ho : I usually start my class at 9:30 a.m., so I leave at 7:30.
It takes about 2 hours from home to school by bus.

Emily : I live in the school dormitory, so I just walk to school.
It's about a ten-minute walk.

02 Vocabulary

1) first thing in the morning 아침에 일어나서 제일먼저
2) go to the bathroom 화장실을 가다
3) take a shower 샤워를 하다
4) cereal 시리얼, 곡류 가공 식품
5) turn on the computer 컴퓨터를 켜다
6) brush one's teeth 양치질을 하다
7) wash one's face 세수를 하다
8) wear toner 스킨을 바르다 (= put on skin toner)

9) wear perfume 향수를 뿌리다 (= put on perfume)
10) leave home 집을 나서다
11) the school dormitory 학교 기숙사
12) walk to school 걸어서 학교에 가다
13) a ten-minute walk 걸어서 10분 걸리는 거리
14) work for the government 공무원이다
15) a housewife 가정주부, 전업주부
16) a sophomore 2학년 (= a second-year student)
17) major in -을 전공하다
18) public administration 행정학
19) an economics major 경제학 전공자
20) as an elective 선택 과목으로
21) a major 전공
22) a double major 복수전공자
23) minor in -을 부전공하다
24) get up 일어나다
25) on weekdays 주중에
26) on weekends 주말에
27) start school 학교 수업을 시작하다
28) finish school 학교 수업을 마치다
29) get to school 학교에 가다/오다 (= go/come to school)
30) take the bus to school 버스를 타고 학교에 가다 (= go to school by bus.)
31) go to work 출근하다
32) drive to work 자가용으로 출근하다 (= go to work by car)
33) ride one's bike to work 자전거로 출근하다 (= go to work by bicycle.)
34) after school 방과 후에
35) do one's homework 숙제를 하다
36) watch TV TV를 보다
37) before bed 취침 전에
38) after work 퇴근 후에
39) go to the gym 헬스클럽/휘트니스센터에 가다
40) lift weights 아령/역기 운동을 하다, 웨이트리프팅을 하다

41) go to bed 잠자리에 들다
42) go to bed with the chickens 일찍 잠자리에 들다
43) a night owl 밤에 늦게 자는 사람 (= a night person)
44) stay up late at night 밤늦게 잠자리에 들다 (= go to bed late at night)
45) at the school cafeteria 학교 구내식당(셀프서비스 식당)에서
46) work part-time 아르바이트를 하다 (= have a part-time job)
47) share an apartment 아파트를 함께 쓰다
48) in my studio apartment 내 원룸아파트에서
49) a boarding house 하숙집
50) vacuum the floor 방바닥을 진공청소기로 청소하다
51) dust the furniture 가구의 먼지를 털다
52) a pet dog 애완견
53) a movie buff 영화광 (= a movie bug)
54) a junk food junkie 패스트푸드광
55) cut down on -을 줄이다
56) go on a diet 다이어트하다
57) eat like a horse 대식가 이다 (= be a heavy eater)
58) health-conscious 건강에 신경 쓰는
59) make it a rule to -하는 것을 규칙으로 삼다
60) take care of -를 돌보다
61) get sick 아프다
62) a morning person (= an early bird/riser)
63) have a sweet tooth 단것을 좋아하다 (= love sweets)
64) have a cavity 충치가 있다
65) be on the wagon 금주 중이다
66) drink like a fish 술고래다
67) be off the wagon 금주를 끝내고 술을 마시다
68) smoke like a chimney 골초다 (= be a heavy smoker)
69) smoke two packs 담배 두 갑을 피우다
70) a chain smoker 줄담배 피우는 사람

영어표현에 나타난 미국문화

Here or to go?

(여기서 드실 건가요, 아니면 가져가실 건가요?)

해외여행을 하다보면 맥도날드 같은 fast-food restaurant에서 햄버거나 커피를 사게 되는 경우가 있는데, 이때 우리가 반드시 듣게 되는 표현이 **"Here or to go?"**이다. 그런데 햄버거 가게에서 주문을 받는 사람들은 하루에도 이루 헤아릴 수 없을 정도로 이 표현을 많이 쓰기 때문에 자동적으로 발음이 빨라질 수밖에 없다. 차라리 긴 문장이라면 그 중에 몇 단어 만으로라도 뜻을 짐작할 수 있겠지만, 몇 개 되지 않는 단어를 빨리 발음해버리면 아예 짐작조차 할 수 없게 되는 것이다. 이렇게 쉬운 단어들로 구성되어 있음에도 불구하고 처음 듣는 사람이라면 미국에서 햄버거 하나도 제대로 사먹기가 곤란할 것이다. 실제로 저자가 10년여 전에 미국에서 햄버거를 사먹기 위해 줄을 서 있었을 때 앞 쪽에서 줄을 서서 주문을 하던 한국 학생이 이 표현을 알아듣지 못하는 바람에 수많은 사람들이 오랫동안 길게 늘어서서 기다려야만 했던 에피소드가 생각난다. 실용영어를 배운다는 것은 그만큼 중요한 것이다.

A: (Is that for) **Here or to go?**
B: **For here. / To go. (여기서 먹을 거예요. / 가져갈 거예요.)**

03 Key Expressions & Application Dialogues

1) A: What do you do?
B: I'm a college student.

2) A: What does your father do?
B: He works for the government.

3) A: What does your mother do?
B: She's a housewife.

4) A: Where do you go to school?
B: I go to Sun Moon University.

5) A: What year are you in?
B: I'm a sophomore.

6) A: What do you major in?
B: I major in public administration.

7) A: Are you an English major?
B: No, I'm an economics major. I'm taking this class as an elective.

8) A: What's your major?
B: I'm a double major in English and economics.

9) A: What do you study at college?
B: Well, I major in English with a minor in Chinese.

10) A: What time do you get up?
B: I usually get up at 6 a.m. on weekdays and at 10:00 a.m. on weekends.

11) A: What time do you start school?
B: I start school at 9:30.

12) A: What time do you finish school?
B: I finish school at 4:20 on Mondays and Tuesdays and at 3:20 on Wednesdays. and Thursdays. I have no class on Fridays.

13) A: How do you get to school?
B: I take the bus to school

14) A: How do you go to school?
B: I take the KTX and the bus to school.

15) A: How does he go to work?
B: He drives to work. Sometimes he rides his bike to work.

16) A: What do you usually do after school?
B: I go home and do my homework.
And sometimes I watch TV before bed.

17) A: What does he do after work?
B: He goes to the gym and lifts weights for an hour.
After that, he goes home and has dinner with his family.

18) A: What time do you go to bed?
B: I go to bed with the chickens. I go to bed around 10:00 p.m.

19) A: Do you go to bed early in the evening?
B: No, I'm a real night owl. I stay up late at night.
I go to bed around 3:00 a.m.

20) A: How many people are there in your family?
B: There are four people in my family.

21) I have my English conversation class on Mondays and Wednesdays

22) I have lunch at 12:30 at the school cafeteria with my friends.

23) I work part-time after school.

24) I share an apartment with my roommate.

25) I cook my own meals in my studio apartment.

26) I live at a boarding house near the campus.

27) I clean the house on Saturdays. I pick up things that are lying around and vacuum the floor. I dust the furniture and the woodwork.

28) I have a pet dog. I take him out for a walk every Sunday.

29) I went grocery shopping with my friend yesterday.

30) I'm going to go see a movie tomorrow. I'm a real movie buff.

31) I'm a real junk food junkie. I'm trying to cut down on hamburgers.

32) I gained 3 kilos. I'm going to go on a diet.

33) You're such a heavy eater. You're eating like a horse. Watch your weight.

34) He's health-conscious. He makes it a rule to go to the gym every day and takes good care of himself. He never gets sick.

35) I'm a morning person. I get up at 5:00 every morning.

36) I have a sweet tooth. I have a cavity.

37) I don't touch alcohol. I'm on the wagon now.

38) My father drinks like a fish. He's off the wagon again.
He drinks almost every day.

39) He smokes like a chimney. He smokes two packs a day.

40) He's a chain smoker.

04 Review : *Fill in the blanks*

1. A: _________ does your mother do?
   B: She's a housewife.

2. A: __________ do you go to school?
   B: I go to Sun Moon University.

3. A: What year are you ________?
   B: I'm a sophomore.

4. I finish school at 4:20 on Mondays and Tuesdays
   and at 3:20 on Wednesdays and Thursdays.
   I have ______ class on Fridays.

5. A: How do you get to school?
   B: I ________ the bus to school

6. A: How does he go to work?
   B: He drives to work. Sometimes he ________ his bike to work.

7. A: What time do you go to bed?
   B: I go to bed with the ___________. I go to bed around 10:00 p.m.

8. A: How many people are there in your family?
   B: __________ ______ four people in my family.

9. I __________ part-time after school.

10. You're such a heavy eater. You're eating like a _________.
    Watch your weight.

Unit 01
Situational English

여가활동 관련표현

01 Conversation

[I'm a real couch potato.]

Joe : What do you usually do in your free time, Fred?
Fred : Well, I go to the gym and work out.
I lift weights and run on the treadmill.
And sometimes I go hiking. I guess I'm a real fitness freak.
Joe : Wow, that's why you look so fit.
Fred : What about you, Joe? What do you do in your free time?
Do you work out?
Joe : No, I don't. I hardly ever exercise.
Actually, **I'm a real couch potato**. I watch TV almost every day.
I really need to exercise, though.
I'm gaining weight, and I'll have to get rid of my love handles.
Fred : Then why don't you go hiking with me next Saturday?
It can really help you lose weight.
Joe : Uh... well, thanks, but I'm not ready to exercise yet.

02 Vocabulary

1) in one's free time 여가시간에
2) work out 운동하다 (= exercise)
3) a fitness freak 운동광
4) a couch potato TV광
5) get rid of -을 제거하다
6) love handles 허릿살
7) go hiking 등산가다

8) lose weight 살을 빼다, 몸무게를 줄이다
9) do sit-ups 윗몸일으키기를 하다
10) do push-ups 팔굽혀펴기를 하다
11) have a green thumb 원예솜씨가 있다 (= be a good gardener)
12) be good at -를 잘하다
13) do gardening 원예를 하다
14) give something two thumbs up 최고 점수를 주다
(= give something one thumb up / give something seven out of ten)
15) a soap opera 연속극
16) give something two thumbs down 최하 점수를 주다
(= give something one thumb down / give something four out of ten)
17) run to the end 끝까지 다 돌아가다
18) edge-of-your-seat 손에 땀을 쥐게 하는
19) a nail-biter 불안하고 초조하게 하는 영화 (= a nail-biting story)
20) eight episodes long 8개 에피소드 분량인
21) a blind spot 난시청 지역
22) a relay tower 중계탑
23) leave the TV on 텔레비전을 켜놓은 채로 자리를 비우다
24) be out of sight 터무니없이 많이 나오다
25) stay tuned to -에 채널고정하다
26) channel-hopping 채널을 이리저리 돌리기
27) move over 비켜서다
28) flip through channels 채널을 이리저리 왔다 갔다 하다
29) the remote 리모콘 (= the remote control)
30) a news flash 짤막한 뉴스 속보
31) the mute button 음소거 버튼
32) a fuzzy picture 뿌옇게 흐린 화면
33) a blurry picture 초점이 맞지 않아 흐릿한 화면
34) a jumpy picture 위 아래로 움직이는 화면
35) a foggy picture 안개가 낀 것처럼 뿌연 화면
36) a snowy picture 화면에 눈이 내리는 것처럼 뿌연 화면
37) take a back seat to -에게 자리를 내 주다

38) get rid of one's tummy 뱃살을 제거하다
39) burn off -을 태워서 없애 버리다
40) the battle of the bulge 살과의 전쟁

03 Key Expressions & Application Dialogues

1) A: How often do you play soccer?
B: Once a week.

2) A: When do you go swimming?
B: Five days a week, from Monday to Friday.

3) A: How many sit-ups do you do every day?
B: I do 30 sit-ups every day. And I do 20 push-ups.

4) A: Wow, you have lots of plants! Do you have a green thumb?
B: Yes, I'm good at gardening. And I do gardening in my free time.

5) A: How did you like the late movie?
B: It was wonderful. I'd give it two thumbs up.

6) A: How was the soap opera?
B: It was terrible. I'd give it two thumbs down.

7) A: The tape ran to the end, and it ran over to the other side of the tape.
B: I bought an empty tape to record on.

8) A: That's an edge-of-your-seat thriller.
B: Right. I was pulled at the edge of my seat while watching it. It's a nail-biter.

9) A: How long is that suspense drama?
B: It's eight episodes long.

10) A: Asan is a blind spot for AFKN.
B: Yes. We need a relay tower.

11) A: Don't leave the TV on. The electric bill is really out of sight.
B: Oh, I just forgot to turn it off.

12) A: Stay tuned to Channel 6. I hate channel-hopping.
B: OK. Move over. You're blocking the view of the television.
You make a better door than you do a window.

13) The 9:00 p.m. news show enjoys the highest audience rating.

14) I was on the phone when this soap opera began.
What did I miss? (= Did I miss anything interesting?)

15) Don't flip through channels. Hand me the remote.

16) While you are watching TV at home, who in your family gets to hold the remote control?

17) There's a news flash floating across the TV screen on Channel 7, which reads, "Seoul's traffic is in red condition due to a heavy snowfall."

18) Why don't you reach for the mute button and kill the sound from the TV?

19) We have a fuzzy picture.
*a blurry/jumpy/foggy/snowy picture.

20) Everything has to take a back seat to your health.

21) I've gained too much weight since I quit smoking.
I really need to get rid of my tummy.

22) Jogging is a good way to burn off some calories.

23) Let's not to lose the battle of the bulge.

24) I do yoga to stay in shape.

25) I go hiking twice a month with my club members.

04 Review : *Put the words in the correct order.*

1. not leave do the on TV
   (TV를 켜둔 채로 자리를 비우지 마세요.)
   ______________________________.

2. give two up thumbs it I'd
   (나는 거기에 최고 점수를 주겠어요.)
   ______________________________.

3. have you thumb do a green
   (당신은 원예 솜씨가 있으세요?)
   ______________________________?

4. thirty I every do day sit-ups
   (나는 매일 윗몸일으키기를 30번씩 합니다.)
   ______________________________.

5. blind AFKN Asan a spot is for
   (아산은 AFKN 난시청지역입니다.)
   ______________________________.

6. bill sight the is really out of electric
   (전기료가 터무니없이 많이 나와요.)
   ______________________________.

7. rid have love handles to get of my I'll
   (나는 허릿살을 제거해야 해요.)
   ______________________________.

8. free time what do do usually in your you
(여가시간에는 대개 뭐하세요?)
____________________________?

9. remote control gets who in family to hold the your
(당신의 집에서는 리모컨(채널) 주도권을 누가 갖고 있어요?)
____?

10. the audience news the highest rating show enjoys 9:00 p.m.
(그 9시 뉴스 프로그램은 최고의 시청률을 자랑합니다.)
____.

영어표현에 나타난 미국문화

Mercurial social dragonfly

(잠시도 한군데에 붙어있지 않고 이리저리 돌아다니기 좋아하는 사람)

수은(水銀 mercury)은 한군데에 정지하지 않고 손으로 집으려고 하면 사방으로 흩어지거나 위치를 이동하는 속성이 있기 때문에, mercurial social dragonfly라고 하면 잠시도 한군데에 붙어있지 않고 활발하게 이리저리 돌아다니기 좋아하는 사람을 가리킨다. 이와 유사한 표현으로 social butterfly라는 말이 있는데, 이것은 여성에게 주로 사용되는 표현이다. 이와는 달리 밖에 나가 돌아다니기 보다는 **집안에 있는 것을 더 좋아하는 사람**을 말할 때는 **homebody**라고 한다. 같은 의미로 **stay-at-home**을 쓰기도 한다.

A: Are you a homebody or a social dragonfly?
(당신은 집안에 있는 것을 더 좋아하세요, 아니면 돌아다니는 것을 좋아하세요?)
B: I guess I'm **a mercurial social dragonfly**.
(저는 잠시도 한군데에 붙어있지 않고 이리저리 돌아다니기를 좋아해요.)

Unit 02 Situational English

영화관람 관련표현

01 Conversation

[Do you like westerns?]

George : What are you going to do after work, Minee?
Minee : Nothing in particular. Why?
George : Why don't we take in a movie? **Do you like westerns?**
Minee : Yes, I'm really into them.
George : That's good. There's *The Good, The Bad, The Weird* showing at CGV now.
Minee : That should be entertaining.
I've heard that it got very good reviews.
George : OK. Let's go see that movie.

02 Vocabulary

1) take in a movie 영화를 보다
(= watch/see/catch a movie/film/flick)
2) westerns 서부영화
3) be into something -를 무척 좋아하다
4) be showing 상영하다/되다 (= be playing/on)
5) be sold out 매진이다
6) the main feature 본 영화
7) the kiosk 매점
8) at the hamburger joint 햄버거 가게(hamburger heaven)에서
9) get a bite (to eat) 간단히 요기하다
(= have/grab a (quick) bite (to eat))
10) be a far cry from -와는 거리가 멀다, -와는 너무 다르다
(= be quite different from)

11) a box-office hit 흥행의 대성공
12) be a big fan of -를 무척 좋아하다, -의 열렬한 팬이다
13) a movie buff 영화광 (= a film buff)
14) come over 멀리서 오다
15) horror films 공포영화 (= horror movies)
16) seats way back in the corner 아주 뒤쪽 구석자리 좌석
17) the next feature 다음 영화 (= the next show)
18) seats in the center 가운데 좌석
19) an action-packed movie 액션영화 (= an action movie)
20) star-studded 대형 스타들이 대거 등장하는
21) walk off with -을 따내다, -을 쉽게 차지하다
22) moviegoing 영화 구경을 자주 가는
23) the intermission 휴게시간
24) the admission 입장료
25) G (= general audiences) 전체 관람가, 연소자 관람가
26) PG (= parental guidance suggested for children) 어린이는 부모 지도가 권고 됨
27) PG-13 (= parental guidance suggested under 13) 13세 미만은 부모 동반해야 입장가
28) R (= restricted admission to only those under 17 accompanied by a parent) 17세 미만은 부모나 보호자 동반해야 입장가
29) NC-17 (= no children under 17 admitted) 17세 이상 관람가, 미성년자 관람불가
30) X-rated 미성년자 관람불가의, 성인용의 (= adults only)

03 Key Expressions & Application Dialogues

1) A: Do you have any seats for the 7:30 show?
B: Awfully sorry. We're all sold out.

2) A: When does the main feature start?
B: It starts at 7:00 p.m. We still have 10 more minutes to kill before the main feature starts.

3) A: Let's get a Coke and a popcorn at the kiosk.
B: OK. I'll go get a couple of Cokes. What size Coke would you like?

4) A: How would you like your popcorn?
Buttered or plain?
B: I'd like hot, buttered popcorn.

5) A: How about getting some snack at the hamburger joint?
B: Good idea. Let's get a bite to eat at the KFC.

6) A: I think that show is a far cry from the original story.
B: Yes, but it's a box-office hit.

7) A: Would you like to catch a flick tonight?
B: Yes, I'd love to.

8) A: I have tickets for the Cho Yongpil's concert tonight.
Would you like to go?
B: Thanks, I'd love to. I'm a big fan of Cho Yongpil.

9) A: We can get tickets for the 9:30 show.
B: That sounds good. So do you want to have dinner at 7:30?

10) A: I'm a real movie buff.
B: Me too. Would you like to watch a movie after work?

11) A: How often do you go to the movies?
B: Once a month, I think.

12) A: Let's take in a movie tonight.
B: Sounds great. Do you have any particular movie in mind?

13) A: I rented a horror movie at the video rental shop this afternoon.
Would you like to come over tonight?
B: Great. I love horror films.

14) A: Good evening. May I help you?
B: Yes. Two tickets for *The good, The Bad, The Weird*, please.
We'd like seats way back in the corner.

15) The next show starts at 9:30, but there are no more seats available.

16) What's playing at the theater?

17) When's the next feature?

18) We prefer seats in the center, please.

19) There's an action-packed movie playing there.

20) This star-studded film has walked off with three Academy Awards.

21) People of all ages are getting the movie-going habit.

22) How long is the intermission?

23) How much is the admission?

24) I'm not familiar with movie ratings, such as G, PG, PG-13, R, and NC-17.

25) That movie is X-rated.

04 Review : *Put the words in the correct order.*

1. movie I a buff real am
(저는 영화광이에요.)
______________________________.

2. big am a of Cho Yongpil I fan
(저는 조용필이 열렬한 팬이에요.)
______________________________.

3. more are seats no available there
(가능한 좌석이 없습니다.)
______________________________.

4. at get a to let's eat the KFC bite
(KFC에서 간단히 요기합시다.)
______________________________.

5. you movies how go often do to the
(영화는 얼마나 자주 보러 가세요?)
______________________________?

6. tonight would to catch you like a flick
(오늘밤에 영화나 한편 볼까요?)
______________________________?

7. in corner like way we'd back the seats
(아주 뒤쪽 구석자리 좌석으로 주세요.)
______________________________.

8. particular you have any in do mind movie
(특별히 마음에 둔 영화가 있습니까?)

____?

9. kiosk a Coke popcorn let's and a at the get
(매점에서 코카콜라와 팝콘을 사도록 합시다.)

____.

10. far original that is a from the story show cry
(그 영화는 원작과는 거리가 멀어요.)

____.

영어표현에 나타난 미국문화

Inside-the-Beltway gossip

(워싱턴정가에서 나도는 세상 돌아가는 이야기)

Washington D.C. 일대를 둘러싼 환상도로(環狀道路)를 일상대화에서 말할 때 미국인들은 the Beltway 또는 the Capital Beltway라고 부르며, inside the Beltway라고 하면 '워싱턴정가에서'라든지 '워싱턴 지배계층사이에서'라는 관용적 표현이 된다. 워싱턴정가(政街)에서 이러쿵저러쿵 나도는 풍문(風聞)이나 세상 돌아가는 이야기를 inside-the-Beltway gossip이라고 한다.

You can enjoy easy access to **all the inside-the-Beltway gossip** by reading this monthly news review. (여러분은 이 월간뉴스논평을 읽음으로써 **워싱턴정가에서 나도는 세상 돌아가는 온갖 이야기**에 쉽게 접할 수 있어요.)

전화대화 관련표현

01 Conversation

[Is he gone for the day?]

Min-ho : SM Plaza. May I help you?
Mary : Yes. I'd like to speak to Mr. Smith, please.
Min-ho : I'm sorry, but he's not in at the moment.
Mary : **Is he gone for the day?**
Min-ho : No. He's just stepped out.
Mary : When do you expect him back?
Min-ho : He'll be back any minute.
May I take a message?
Mary : No, thanks. I'll call back later.

02 Vocabulary

1) at the moment 지금 (= now)
2) be gone 가버리다
3) step out 잠깐 자리를 비우다
4) expect someone back -가 돌아올 것이라고 예상하다
5) be back 돌아오다
6) any minute 곧 (= soon)
7) on business 사업차, 출장차
8) be off 쉬는 날이다
9) ring a bell 생각이 나다
10) escape 잊혀 지다, 생각나지 않다
11) frequently dialed numbers 자주 거는 전화번호

12) burn up the line 전화통화를 오래하다
13) take a back seat 양보하다
14) at a bad time 좋지 않은 때에
15) keep ringing -계속해서 울리다
16) be left unanswered 전화를 받지 않다
17) screen one's calls -의 전화를 가려 받다
18) look up -을 찾아보다
19) the phone directory 전화번호부 (= the phone book)
20) be listed 목록에 있다
21) store -을 저장하다
22) sign up for -에 등록하다
23) spit out -을 뱉어내다
24) be out of range 통화권을 이탈하다
25) turn off -을 끄다
26) vibrate mode 진동모드
27) run out 소모되다
28) illegal 불법의
29) behind the wheel 운전중에 (= while driving)
30) hang up -을 끊다

03 Key Expressions & Application Dialogues

1) A: May I speak to Mr. Kim?
B: He is out on business.

2) A: Can I talk with Mr. Kim?
B: He can't come to the phone right now. He's in a meeting.

3) A: Is Mr. Kim in?
B: He's off today.

4) A: When can I expect you back?
B: Expect me when you see me.

5) A: May I ask who's calling?
B: This is Mary Smith at Korean Air.

6) A: She gave me her phone number. Her phone number is 530-1031.
B: That number doesn't ring a bell.

7) A: Could you give me his phone number?
B: His phone number escapes me. That's my frequently dialed number, though.

8) A: We've been burning up the lines for about 10 minutes.
It's costing you a lot.
B: That's OK. Money has to take a backseat to our friendship.

9) A: I hope I'm not calling you at a bad time.
B: That's OK. Now I'm in the middle of reading.

10) A: The bell keeps ringing, but the phone is left unanswered.
B: I think he is screening his calls.

11) A: Look up her phone number in the phone directory.
B: Well, I don't think her number is listed.

13) A: I'm going to sign up for the mobile phone service. What wireless company are you with?
B: I have KTF.

12) I stored 15 frequently dialed phone numbers in my cellphone.

14) Long time, no talk. (= Long time, no hear.)

15) This cardphone is spitting out my phone card.

16) This pay phone only takes coins.
(= It's a coin-only pay phone.)

17) My cellphone is out of range.
(= I'm not in the service area any longer.)

18) Please turn your cellphone off.

19) Set/Put your cell phone to/on vibrate mode.
(= Set/Put your cell to/on vibrate.)

20) This phone card has only 720 won left on it.

21) My phone card has almost run out.

22) It's illegal to use a cellphone behind the wheel.
Please hang up and drive.

23) My phone calls are cut off mid-sentence due to low battery.

24) My phone battery is dead. Now, let me replace it with a backup battery.

25) Awfully sorry to call you at this late hour.

04 Review : *Put the words in the correct order.*

1. the he for day is gone
(그분은 아주 퇴근하셨나요?)
_________________________?

2. out my range cellphone is of
(여기는 핸드폰이 안 터지는 지역이에요.)
_________________________________.

3. fingers the let do your walking
(갈 것 없이 전화로 하세요.)
___________________________________.

4. cellphone vibrate your to mode set
(핸드폰을 진동모드로 해두세요.)
_______________________________________.

5. like to Mr. Smith to please I'd speak
(김 선생님 좀 바꿔주세요.)
____.

6. out this is phone spitting cardphone my card
(이 공중전화는 내 전화카드를 밀어내고 있어요.)
____.

7. late I'm call hour at awfully to you sorry this
(이렇게 늦은 시간에 전화를 드려서 죄송합니다.)
____.

8. behind illegal to a use it's the cellphone wheel
(운전 중에 전화하는 것은 불법입니다.)

____.

9. sign for going service to up the I'm phone mobile
(저는 이동전화 서비스에 가입할 작정이에요.)

____.

10. not number in listed is phone the phone her directory
(그녀의 전화번호는 전화번호부에 나와 있지 않아요.)

____.

영어표현에 나타난 미국문화

Contiguous United States

(미국 본토)

미국 전체 50개 주들 가운데 하와이와 알래스카를 제외한 워싱턴 D.C.포함하여 나머지 48개주를 미국본토 또는 미국대륙이라고 하는데, 미국인들은 **the (48) contiguous United States**, 또는 **the (48) continental United States**, 그리고 미 군사 용어로 **CONUS**라고 표현한다.

You get what you pay for. This offer is valid only in **the 48 contiguous United States**. You'll incur no purchase obligation whatever during your 90-day trial membership. We always cherish bargain-loving Americans.
(제 값은 제가 지니고 있는 겁니다(물건은 구매할 때 돈이 들어간 만큼 모두 제값을 합니다). 이번 가격혜택은 **미 대륙 48개주(미국본토)**에서만 유효합니다. 90일간 시험삼아 실시하는 회원자격기간 동안에 고객들은 하등의 상품구입의무를 지지 않습니다. 저희는 염가세일을 좋아하는 미국인들을 항시 고귀하게 모십니다.)

날씨 관련표현

01 Conversation

[We're having perfect skiing weather today.]

Mini : What's the weather like today?

Steve : It's arctic weather with heavy snow. The weatherman said that it would be snowy today. **We're having perfect skiing weather today.**

Mini : Oh, really?

Steve : We're going to have a snowbound weekend.

Mini : No problem. We can put the chains on and make it to one of the countryside ski resorts.

Steve : Sounds great. Now we have already had an inch of snow.

Mini : Why don't we monitor weather reports before we get started on a trip to a ski resort?

Steve : Why not? Turn on the TV so that we can check out the weather channel.

02 Vocabulary

1) the weatherman 기상통보관
2) arctic weather 극한의 날씨
3) snowbound weather 눈 때문에 꼼짝 못하는 날씨
4) the flu 독감 (= the influenza)
5) catch cold 감기에 걸리다
6) catching 옮기 쉬운, 감염성의
7) have a fever 열이 나다
8) have a sore throat 목이 아프다
9) hang on and on 영 떨어지지 않다

10) frigid 무척 추운 (= freezing cold)
11) bundle up 옷을 여러 겹으로 끼워 입다
12) sub-zero temperature 영하의 날씨 (= minus temperature)
13) the weather forecast 일기예보
14) break 누그러지다, 한풀 꺾이다
15) have a cold 감기에 걸리다
16) have a frog in one's throat 목이 쉬다
17) clear one's throat 목청을 가다듬다, 헛기침 하다
18) soaked 흠뻑 젖은
19) rain cats and dogs 비가 억수같이 내리다 (= rain heavily)
20) today's windchill factor 오늘의 체감온도
21) duck 몸을 획/숙여서 피하다
22) a freeze 몹시 추운 날씨
23) a bitterly cold day 살을 에는 듯이 추운 날
24) a scorcher 몹시 더운 날씨 (= a sizzler)
25) turn up -을 켜다
26) turn down -을 끄다
27) yesterday's low 어제의 최저 기온
28) tomorrow's high 내일의 최고 기온
29) come to an end 끝나다
30) the rainy spell 장마 (= the rainy season)

03 Key Expressions & Application Dialogues

1) A: We're having perfect hiking weather.
   B: Why don't we go hiking then?

2) A: We're having flu weather. Ahchoo! Now I'm catching cold.
   B: Brrr! Is it catching?

3) A: My nose is runny and I have a fever. And I have a sore throat.
B: Stay indoors! The bad cold that's been going around recently hangs on and on.

4) A: What's the weather like outside?
B: It's frigid outside, so I don't want to move an inch.
Why don't we bundle up?

5) A: We are going to have sub-zero temperatures tomorrow.
B: According to the weather forecast, the cold weather is going to break next week.

6) A: Spring is in the air. The weather is perfect.
B: Yes. The weather couldn't be better.
It's too nice a day to be inside.

7) A: The snow changed to rain.
B: Really? Let's wait the rain out.

8) A: Mom, I have a bad cold.
And I've got a frog in my throat.
B: I think you have to clear your throat.

9) A: We expect some mild days in a couple of weeks.
B: It won't be long before spring is here.

10) A: It's lovely weather for ducks.
B: It sure is. I got soaked to the skin in the rain.

11) It's raining cats and dogs.

12) Today's windchill factor is five degrees below zero.

13) Duck/Get under my umbrella.

14) It's another freeze today. (= It's another bitterly cold day.)

15) It's another scorcher today. (= It's another sizzler today.)

16) Yesterday's temperature reached sauna levels.

17) The cold/hot weather has already broken.

18) Did the cold/hot weather break?

19) Please turn up/down the air-conditioning.

20) What was yesterday's low?

21) What is tomorrow's high?

22) Has the hot/cold weather come to an end yet?

23) The rainy spell/season has just started.

24) It looks like rain/snow.

25) It looks like a storm coming.

04 Review : *Put the words in the correct order.*

1. my duck umbrella under
   (내 우산 속으로 들어오세요.)
   ______________________________.

2. like what today weather the is
   (오늘 날씨는 어떻습니까?)
   ______________________________.

3. frog I in throat a my got have
   (나는 목이 잠겼어요.)
   ______________________________.

4. windchill today's factor is what
   (오늘의 체감온도는 얼마예요?)
   ______________________________?

5. bad on cold and hangs on the
   (그 심한 감기는 잘 떨어지지 않아요.)
   ______________________________.

6. it so frigid up outside bundle is
   (바깥 날씨가 매우 추우니까 옷을 두툼하게 입으세요.)
   ______________________________.

7. rain the got to skin in I the soaked
   (나는 비에 흠뻑 젖었어요.)
   ______________________________.

8. yet rainy an come the spell to end has
(이제 장마가 끝났나요?)

____?

9. perfect having skiing we're today weather
(오늘은 스키타기에 아주 좋은 날씨예요.)

____.

10. have temperatures we going tomorrow sub-zero to are
(내일은 영하의 날씨가 될 것입니다.)

____.

영어표현에 나타난 미국문화

Rain was pouring down from the night sky
at a rate that would have alarmed Noah.
(밤하늘에서 엄청난 속도로 비가 퍼붓고 있었다.)

비가 무섭게 쏟아지고 있다는 말을 강조하기 위하여, 방주(Noah's Ark)로 홍수에서 인류의 최후를 구해낸 "노아를 놀라게 할 만한 속도로" 하늘에서 비가 쏟아지고 있다고 표현한 것이다. **지금 하늘에서 비가 무섭게 쏟아지고 있다**는 말을 "**Rain is pouring from the sky at a rate that would alarm Noah.**"라고 하면 아주 멋진 표현이 될 것이다.

아울러, "비가 억수같이 쏟아지고 있다"라는 영어 표현으로 "It's raining cats and dogs."라는 표현도 함께 기억하면 유용할 것이다. "It never rains but it pours."는 비가 오지 않다가도 일단 왔다 하면 퍼붓는다는 의미로 우리가 흔히 말하는 "불행은 겹쳐온다"는 영어 표현이다.

Unit 05

Situational English

헤어숍 이용 관련표현

01 Conversation

[How would you like your hair done?]

Beautician : **How would you like your hair done?**
Jessica : I'd like a straight permanent, please.
I don't like my thick, stiff hair.
Beautician : All right, ma'am. Shall I fix it the way you had it before?
Jessica : Yes. I'd like my hair long, and I want to have it tinted. I love brunette.
Beautician : Okay. And you, sir?
George : I'd like my hair long. Just a styling, please.
Some hairs keep sticking up.
Beautician : All right, sir. But I think the top needs thinning.
George : That's OK. I want to leave it the way it is.

02 Vocabulary

1) a straight permanent 스트레이트 파마
2) thick, stiff hair 두껍고 뻣뻣한 머릿결
3) tinted 염색한
4) brunette 갈색머리
5) stick up 쭈뼛하게 일어서다
6) thinning 머리숱치기
7) pick up -을 돋보이게 하다
8) patronize -를 단골로 하다
9) a beauty shop 뷰티숍 (= a beauty parlor)
10) flow down 흘러내리다

11) part one's hair 가르마를 타다
12) brush back 빗으로 빗어 넘기다
13) clippers 머리 깎는 기계
14) scissors 가위
15) even out 고르게/편평하게 하다
16) salt-and-pepper 희끗희끗한 (= gray)
17) thin out 머리숱을 치다
18) a natural hairdo 자연스러운 헤어스타일
19) perfume 향수
20) wear lipstick 립스틱을 바르다
21) too loud 너무 야한
22) clip-on earrings 클립형 귀걸이
23) wear heavy makeup 짙은 화장을 하다
24) be congenial to makeup 화장이 잘 받는
25) bleached 탈색한 (= highlighted)
26) platinum-blonde hair 은빛 도는 금발머리
27) shoulder-length hair 어깨까지 오는 길이의 머리
28) dark-brown eyes 눈동자가 검은 눈
29) make layers 머리를 층지게 자르다
30) split ends 끝이 갈라진 머리

03 Key Expressions & Application Dialogues

1) A: Your haircut picks up your looks.
B: Really? Thank you.

2) A: I need a straight perm.
B: What beauty shop do you patronize the most?

3) A: The beauty shop has the best perms in town.
B: You bet. I also had a perm put in my hair at that beauty parlor.

4) A: I hate my hair flowing down on my forehead.
B: OK. Let me cut it short.

5) A: Do you part your hair on the left or on the right?
B: Just brush it back, please.

6) A: Hair cut, sir?
B: Yes. Clippers in the back only. Scissors but no clippers on the sides.

7) A: Even out the top, but not too short on top.
B: Very well, sir.

8) A: I'll give you a shampoo, ma'am. Please follow me.
B: Okay.

9) A: Tell me about Jackie. What does she look like?
B: Well, she has long blonde hair flowing down her back.

10) A: Oh, my! My hair is salt-and-pepper now.
B: Yes. But better gray than gone.

11) A: How would you like your hair?
B: Thin it out on the back of my head.

12) A: What kind of hair style would you like?
B: I'd like a natural hairdo.

13) A: What kind of perfume do you wear?
B: Chanel.

14) A: Wear this color lipstick, please.
B: Red color lipstick is too loud for the ceremony.

15) A: Don't you wear lipstick?
B: Yes. I often wear lipstick in a purple shade.

16) A: How do I look with these clip-on earrings?
B: You look great, and they really pick up your looks.

17) Don't wear heavy makeup to the interview.

18) Jackie's face is congenial to makeup.

19) I had my hair bleached/highlighted.

20) Did you shampoo your hair before coming here?

21) Mary has platinum-blonde hair.

22) Nicole has shoulder-length hair.

23) You have beautiful dark-brown eyes.

24) Can you make layers in the back?

25) You have split ends. How about a trim and then a light perm?

04 Review : *Put the words in the correct order.*

1. you hair how like your would
(머리를 어떻게 해 드릴까요?)
_______________________________?

2. haircut looks your up your picks
(당신은 이발하니까 얼굴이 돋보이네요.)
_______________________________.

3. part do left on you hair the your
(당신은 머리가르마를 왼쪽으로 타세요?)
_______________________________?

4. back in can you layers the make
(머리 뒤쪽을 층지게 잘라 주시겠어요?)
_______________________________?

5. kind wear perfume what of do you
(당신은 어떤 향수를 쓰세요?)
_______________________________?

6. it of on my thin out the back head
(머리 뒤쪽에 숱 좀 쳐주세요.)
_______________________________.

7. makeup interview wear not heavy to the do
(인터뷰에는 화장을 짙게 하고 가지마세요.)
_______________________________.

8. earrings these I how look with clip-on do
(이 클립형 귀걸이가 저에게 잘 어울리나요?)
____?

9. do patronize what shop you the most beauty
(어느 미용실을 단골로 다니세요?)
____?

10. blonde down she long hair flowing her back has
(그녀는 등 뒤로 흘러내리는 긴 금발머리를 하고 있어요.)
____.

영어표현에 나타난 미국문화

Manicure and Nail Polish

(손톱화장과 매니큐어)

손톱화장(fingernail makeup)에 사용하는 광택제를 우리는 흔히 「매니큐어」라고 부르는데, 영어로 **manicure**라고 하면 손톱에 바르는 화장품을 가리키는 말이 아니라 **「손톱화장」**을 의미한다. 다시 말해서, 손톱 다듬기부터 영양주기, 메니큐어바르기, 네일아트 등의 모든 과정을 포함하는 손톱관리 즉, 손톱화장을 의미하는 것이다. (물론, 손톱 뿐만 아니라 손 전체의 관리를 포함한다.) 그래서 **손톱화장에 바르는 광택제**는 영어로 manicure가 아니라 **nail polish**라고 해야 정확한 영어표현이 된다. 참고적으로, 요즘에 여성들 사이에서는 손톱화장뿐만 아니라 **발톱화장**도 유행하고 있는데, 발톱화장을 영어로는 **pedicure**라고 한다. (참고로, 어원은 라틴어의 *pes* ("foot") + *cura* ("cure")이다.)

그런데, 영어로 manicure라는 단어가 라틴어의 *manos* ("hand")와 *cura* ("cure")라는 단어의 결합이기 때문에 "hair"라는 의미가 전혀 없음에도 불구하고 요즘에 한국의 헤어숍에서 손상된 머리에 해주는 헤어영양코팅의 일종으로 메니큐어라는 말을 사용하고 있다. 아마도 손톱영양코팅에 사용하는 염색제인 헤나(henna)를 머리손질에서 사용하기 때문에 생긴 용어인 것 같다.

Unit 06 Situational English

의류 쇼핑 관련표현

01 Conversation

[It's a little too tight for me.]

Jina : Excuse me, do you have this jacket in size 55?
Clerk : Just a moment, please. Oh, Here's one in that size. Would you like to try it on?
Jina : Yes. Oh, **it's a little too tight for me.** I need a little more ease across the chest.
Clerk : May I interest you in this plaid jacket then?
Jina : Okay. Let me try it on. It fits me very well.
Clerk : It looks good on you. It's a perfect fit.
Jina : Thank you. I'll take it.

02 Vocabulary

1) too tight 너무 꽉 끼는
2) ease 넉넉함, 여분
3) interest -에게 흥미를 갖게 하다
4) a plaid jacket 격자무늬 자켓
5) a perfect fit 안성맞춤
6) in a larger size 더 큰 치수로
7) in a different color 다른 색상으로
8) clothes shopping 의류 쇼핑
9) browse -을 둘러보다
10) a refund 환불
11) the sales slip 영수증 (= the receipt)

12) the bottom price 최저가
13) haggle 흥정하다
14) go by the price tag 정찰제로 하다
15) too steep 너무 비싼
16) come down 가격을 깎아주다
17) a steal 헐값, 공짜나 다름없는 가격
18) take one's measurements 치수를 재다
19) a fitting 가봉
20) corduroy pants 골덴 바지
21) wrinkle-prone 구김이 잘 가는
22) wrinkle-free 구김이 잘 안가는
23) stay creased 바지의 주름이 그대로 유지되다
24) apiece 하나에
25) wash-and-wear 빨아서 다림질 필요 없이 입을 수 있는
26) see-through 속이 훤히 비치는
27) clotheshorse 옷 사는데 돈을 많이 쓰는 사람
28) four-way stretch 사방 스판
29) one-size-fits-all 프리 사이즈
30) custom-tailored 맞춤의

03 Key Expressions & Application Dialogues

1) A: Do you have this in a larger size?
B: Yes, but in a different color.

2) A: Where are you going?
B: I'm going clothes shopping in Myoungdong.

3) A: May I help you, ma'am?
B: No, thank you. I'm just browsing.

4) A: Can I help you?
B: I'm being helped. Thanks anyway.

5) A: Excuse me. I'd like a refund on this shirt.
B: OK. Do you have the sales slip?

6) A: What's your bottom price?
B: We don't haggle over the price at this store.
We strictly go by the price tag.

7) A: That's too steep. Can you come down a little?
B: What's your budget?

8) A: Any better price?
B: What price range do you have in mind?

9) A: I bought this jacket for 10,000 won.
B: Wow! That's a steal.

10) A: Let me take your measurements.
B: When will it be ready for a fitting?

11) A: I think these corduroy pants are wrinkle-prone and they bag easily at the knees.
B: No. They are wrinkle-free pants and stay creased for a couple of weeks.

12) A: How much do you charge for these shirts?
B: They are 10,000 won apiece. They are wash-and-wear shirts.

13) A: I don't know what to wear to the party.
B: Don't wear a see-through skirt to the party.

14) A: Don't you wear socks?
B: No. I go sockless in my slip-on shoes in summer.

15) Jane is a clotheshorse.
(= Jane spends a lot of money on clothes.)

16) I'd like to exchange this.

17) Don't you think this jacket is too showy?

18) Come in and treat yourself to a browse.

19) These jeans feature four-way stretch for comfort.

20) Your shirttail is hanging out. (= Your shirttail is sticking out.)

21) Do you have this shirt in blue?

22) This T-shirt is one-size-fits-all wear.

23) Is it ready-made or custom-tailored.

24) I always have my suits custom-tailored.

25) The saleslady lowered the price on the trench coat, and it was difficult for me to refuse.

04 Review : *Put the words in the correct order.*

1. on it would to try you like
(그것을 한번 입어 보실래요?)
______________________________.

2. tight for is a too me it little
(그것은 내기 입기에 좀 끼어요.)
______________________________.

3. this like a on refund shirt I'd
(이 셔츠를 환불받고 싶습니다.)
______________________________.

4. go we price by the tag strictly
(저희가게에서는 엄격히 정찰제로 합니다.)
______________________________.

5. have size a do this in larger you
(이거 더 큰 사이즈로 있어요?)
______________________________?

6. ready fitting will be for a when it
(언제 쯤 가봉이 됩니까?)
______________________________?

7. have in you what range mind do price
(얼마 정도의 가격을 생각하고 계세요?)
______________________________?

8. yourself and come in to a browse treat
(들어와서 편히 구경하세요.)

____.

9. showy jacket think this is too you don't
(이 재킷이 너무 화려한 것 같지 않아요?)

____?

10. shopping Myoungdong I going clothes in am
(나는 명동으로 의류 쇼핑하러 가고 있어요.)

____.

영어표현에 나타난 미국문화

Money talks!

(돈이면 안 되는 것이 없어요.)

"Money talks."라고 하면 돈이면 안 되는 것이 없다든지 또는 돈이 힘을 발휘한다는 금언(maxim)이다. 미국의 어느 쇼핑센터 입구에 나붙은 **"If money talks, we shout."(돈이 힘이 있다면 저희업소에서는 돈이 제대로 힘을 발휘해요.)**라는 문구가 퍽 인상적이었다. 돈이 talk한다면 자기네 판매업소야말로 말한다는 영향력의 강도가 낮은 talk의 정도가 아니라 고함친다는 뜻의 강도가 한 단계 높은 shout를 한다는 것이니 돈이 제 위력을 발휘하는—매장가격이 저렴하여 돈의 구매력이 아주 큰—업소라는 말이다. 취업인터뷰를 하러가는 여성들은 화장을 고치면서 **"Beauty talks."(아름다워야 점수를 따요.)**라는 말을 할 것이다.

Unit 07 Situational English

의류세탁 관련표현

01 Conversation

[Is this hand-washable?]

Laundryman : May I help you?
Moon-sook : Yes. I spilt ink on this blouse. **Is this hand-washable?**
Laundryman : I'm afraid not. I think it needs dry cleaning.
Moon-sook : When will it be ready?
Laundryman : It'll be ready by tomorrow morning.
Why don't you double-check on that?
Moon-sook : Okay. I'll call you before coming to pick it up.
Laundryman : We'll do our best to get the stain out.
Moon-sook : Thank you. See you later.

02 Vocabulary

1) spill -을 쏟다
2) hand-washable 손세탁이 가능한
3) double-check 재확인하다
4) a stain 얼룩 (= a spot/mark)
5) get something out -을 제거하다 (= remove)
6) pick up -을 찾다, -을 가지러 오다
7) at your convenience 당신이 편리한 시간에
8) the claim check 확인증
9) do the laundry 세탁하다
10) leak 새다
11) ruined 망친, 얼룩진

12) shrink 줄어들다
13) the color may run 색이 빠질 가능성이 있다
14) fussy 까다로운
15) a laundromat 동전세탁소/세탁기, 빨래방 (= a coin-op laundry)
15) the change machine 동전 교환기
16) be ripped at the seams 솔기가 터지다
17) drop off -을 맡기다
18) on one's way to work 출근길에
19) make deliveries 배달을 해 주다
20) faded 색이 바랜
21) a laundry shop 세탁소, 빨래방 (= a coin laundry)
22) let something out -의 품을 좀 늘리다
23) loose 헐렁한 (= baggy)
24) take something in -의 품을 좀 줄이다
25) have something shortened -의 길이를 좀 줄이다
26) have something lengthened -의 길이를 좀 늘리다
27) hand-wash -을 손빨래하다
28) come off 잘 빠지다
29) pick up a lot of dirt 먼지가 많이 붙다
30) get wrinkled easily 쉽게 구김이 가다

03 Key Expressions & Application Dialogues

1) A: I'd like to have this suit dry-cleaned. How long will it take?
B: Well, you can pick it up anytime after five the day after tomorrow.

2) A: What time shall I come to pick it up tomorrow?
B: At your convenience.

3) A: I'm here to pick up my laundry. Here's the claim check.
B: OK. Here you are.

4) A: I'm awfully sorry. I spilt my grape juice on the carpet.
B: No problem.

5) A: Are you going to do the laundry?
B: No. I'm going to have it dry-cleaned.

6) A: My ball-point pen leaked all over my shirt.
B: Your shirt is ruined. That's too bad.
Why don't you go to the cleaner's to have it dry-cleaned?

7) A: This shirt has a mark here. Can you remove it?
B: Sure. We should be able to. Don't worry!

8) A: This coat won't shrink, but the color may run if washed.
B: Oh, my goodness. The problem is that my boy is very fussy about what he wears.

9) A: We did our best to get the stain out.
B: Wow, it has completely gone.
You did a good job on it. Thank you.

10) A: I have a lot of laundry to do.
B: Me too. Hey, there's a laundromat in this building.
Why don't we go there after dinner?

11) A: Do you have some coins for this laundromat?
B: No, but we can use the change machine over there in the corner.

12) A: May I help you?
B: Yes. My jeans are ripped at the seams.

13) A: Will you drop off these coats at the dry cleaner's?
B: No problem. I'll drop them off on my way to work.

14) Do you make deliveries?

15) I'd like it delivered to my apartment.

16) My blue jeans got faded from washing.

17) What laundry shop do you patronize the most?
(= What laundry shop do you go to regularly?)

18) This coat is too tight across the chest.
Please let it out.

19) This coat is too loose/baggy. Please take it in.

20) The legs of my pants are a little too long.
I'd like (to have) them shortened.

21) The legs of my pants are a little too short.
I'd like (to have) them lengthened.

22) You have to hand-wash it.

23) I have a spot on my jacket.

24) This coffee stain won't come off.

25) This material picks up a lot of dirt and gets wrinkled easily.

04 Review : *Put the words in the correct order.*

1. if the run washed may color
(물빨래를 하면 색깔이 바랠지도 모릅니다.)
_______________________________.

2. laundry to pick I here up my am
(세탁물 맡긴 것을 찾으러 왔습니다.)
_______________________________.

3. the to laundry are going do you
(빨래하시려는 거예요?)
_______________________________?

4. come this won't off coffee stain
(이 커피얼룩은 잘 빠지지 않아요.)
_______________________________.

5. are my the jeans seams ripped at
(제 데님바지의 솔기가 터졌어요.)
_______________________________.

6. picks this of dirt material up a lot
(이 재질은 먼지가 많이 붙어요.)
_______________________________.

7. in is this there a laundromat building
(이 건물에 동전세탁소가 하나 있어요.)
_______________________________.

8. like suit dry-cleaned I this would have to
(이 정장을 드라이클리닝해주세요.)

____.

9. would delivered to my I like it apartment
(제 아파트까지 배달해 주시면 좋겠습니다.)

____.

10. best stain we our to do the out will get
(나는 최선을 다해 그 얼룩을 빼겠습니다.)

____.

영어표현에 나타난 미국문화

PURR-fect Car Repair Shop

(엔진소리가 제대로 나도록 완벽한 수리를 해주는 카센터)

차량의 정비상태가 양호하여 엔진소리가 조용하고도 고르게 나는 것을 들으면 미국인들은 **"This car purrs like a kitten."(이 차는 엔진소리가 고르고 부드러워요.)**이라고 말한다. 직역하면 "이 차는 새끼고양이처럼 그르릉거린다."라는 말인데, 고양이가 밥을 실컷 먹고 난 후에 행복에 겨워 양지바른 곳에 쪼그리고 앉아 그르릉거리는 소리를 내듯이 엔진소리가 고르고 부드럽다는 말이다. "Vroom! Vrrrroooom! ***Purr***rrrr!(부르릉 부르릉 부르릉 부르릉, 동 동 동 동!)"하면서 엔진소리가 고르게 날 정도로 ***per***fect car repair(완벽한 차량수리)를 해주는 카센터라는 뜻으로 **PURR-fect**라는 신조어를 만들어낸 것이다.

Unit 08

Situational English

길안내 관련표현

01 Conversation

[Only sub-compact cars are allowed angle parking at the curb.]

George : Could you draw me a map? Please use some landmarks and give me directions.

Min-joo : I see. Is this your first time here?

George : Yes, I'm a stranger here myself.

Min-joo : Do you have transportation available?

George : Sure. I rented a car.

Min-joo : That full-size sedan over there?

George : Exactly.

Min-joo : You know, **only sub-compact cars are allowed angle parking at the curb**.

George : Really? I didn't know that. Thank you for the tip.

02 Vocabulary

1) landmarks 이정표
2) a stranger 처음 온 사람 (= a newcomer)
3) transportation 교통편
4) available 가능한
5) rent a car 자동차를 빌리다
6) a full-size sedan 대형 자동차
7) sub-compact cars 경차
8) angle parking 개구리 주차
9) the curb 연석

10) the tip 도움말
11) take the right/wrong way 길을 제대로/잘못 들어서다
12) pick up -을 차로 마중 나가다/나오다
13) go straight ahead 똑바로 직진하다
14) the bus-only lane 버스 전용차선
15) nearby 근처에
16) pick up -을 중간에서 태우다
17) hitchhikers 자동차 편승 여행자
18) nowadays 요즈음에는
19) take rides from strangers 모르는 사람 차를 얻어 타다
20) reckless 무모한
21) cross the median 중앙선을 침범하다/넘다
22) a jay walker 도로를 무단횡단 하는 사람
23) the overhead crosswalk 육교
24) the traffic light 교통신호등
25) thumb a ride 자동차 편승 여행을 하다 (= hitchhike)
26) the information desk 안내데스크
27) miss 놓치다, 못보고 지나치다
28) have difficulty -ing -하는데 어려움을 겪다
29) get off 내리다
30) have a good memory for directions 길눈이 밝다

03 Key Expressions & Application Dialogues

1) A: Am I taking the right way to the Olympic Stadium?
B: No. You are taking the wrong way.

2) A: What floor is the office on?
B: It's on the 7th floor. Take the elevator to the 7th floor and turn right.

3) A: Shall I pick you up there?
B: No, thank you. I can get there by myself.

4) A: Are you a newcomer to Tangjeong?
B: Yes. I just got here.

5) A: How do I get to the post office?
B: Go straight ahead for two blocks and turn to the right at the stop light.

6) A: This is the bus-only lane.
B: Oh, I just forgot. We are not allowed to drive in a bus-only lane on Sundays.

7) A: Is there a landmark nearby?
B: Yes. There's a bank on your right.

8) A: People hate to pick up hitchhikers nowadays.
B: That's true. And I don't like to take rides from strangers.

9) A: Reckless drivers are crossing the median.
B: Yes. Do defensive driving.

10) A: Hey, don't be a jay walker. It's very dangerous and illegal.
B: OK. Let's use the overhead crosswalk.

11) A: Why don't we thumb a ride?
B: No, I don't think it's a good idea. It's too dangerous.

12) Wait for the traffic light to change.

13) The office is one floor up.

14) You are on the wrong floor.

15) Please check at the information desk.

16) When is the soonest you can make it here?

17) You shouldn't have any difficulty finding the railway station.
You can't miss it.

18) Please get off at the next stop.

19) What street am I on now?

20) Where am I now?

21) I have a good memory for directions.

22) I have difficulty finding my way around.

23) It's just three blocks that way.

24) You'll come to a Y-intersection, and angle to the left/right.

25) Follow your nose. (= Go straight ahead.)

04 Review : *Put the words in the correct order.*

1. is a nearby there landmark
   (근처에 중요시설물이 있나요?)
   ______________________________?

2. the floor you on wrong are
   (층수를 잘못 찾아오셨어요.)
   ______________________________.

3. overhead the use crosswalk let's
   (보행자용 육교를 이용합시다.)
   ______________________________.

4. I post do to get the how office
   (우체국에 가려면 어떻게 가야 하나요?)
   ______________________________.

5. time is first in this L.A. your
   (L.A.는 이번이 처음이세요?)
   ______________________________?

6. have you transportation do available
   (차 같은 교통편은 있어요?)
   ______________________________?

7. memory have directions a for I good
   (저는 길눈이 밝아요.)
   ______________________________.

8. information please desk check the at
(안내데스크에 확인하세요.)

______________________________________.

9. allowed at the curb sub-compact are angle only parking cars
(경차들만이 연도(沿道)에 개구리주차가 허용됩니다.)

____.

10. in not allowed drive are a lane to Sundays we bus-only on
(일요일에는 버스전용차선에서 달리면 안 됩니다.)

____.

영어표현에 나타난 미국문화

Just like going to the dentist

(죽는 것만큼이나 싫은)

충치라던가 구강관련 문제로 한번이라도 치과 의사의 치료를 받아 본 경험이 있는 사람이라면 누구나 두 번 다시 치과(dental clinic)에 가기를 꺼려할 것이다. 특히, 치과의사가 드르륵 드르륵 환자의 치아를 드릴로 갈아내기(tooth drilling)라도 하면 몸이 움츠러질 정도로 심한 공포와 통증을 느끼게 되니 치과병원에 다시 간다는 것이 죽는 것만큼 싫다는 말을 하고도 남을 것 같다. 그래서 미국인들은 아주 하기 싫은 일을 말할 때, 치과에 가는 것과 같은 기분이라고 말한다.

미국 연방 준비제도 이사회(the Federal Reserve Board)의 의장(Chairman)이었던 Alan Greenspan(대외공식명칭: Federal Reserve Chairman)이 상원 청문회에서, **"Coming up here** (for a Senate hearing) **is like going to the dentist."(여기** 상원청문회에 **오기가 죽는 것만큼이나 싫어요.)** 라고 한 말은 치과진료에 대한 미국인들의 혐오증을 여실히 나타내고 있다.

은행업무 관련표현

01 Conversation

[Is there an ATM around here?]

Steve : Excuse me. **Is there an ATM around here?**
Min-ji : Pardon me?
Steve : Is there an automated teller machine near here?
Min-ji : Oh, yes, there's one at the far end of this lobby. But the ATM machine is out of service at 3:30 p.m.
Steve : Oh, really? Isn't round-the-clock service available at the ATM?
Min-ji : No, not that I know of.

02 Vocabulary

1) an ATM 현금 자동 입출금기 (= an automated teller machine)
2) the far end 맨 끝쪽
3) round-the-clock service 24시간 사용
4) the PIN 비밀번호 (= the personal identification number)
5) insert -을 삽입하다
6) the cash card 현금 인출 카드
7) withdraw -을 인출하다
8) lastly 마지막으로, 끝으로
9) take out -을 꺼내다
10) the statement 거래명세표
11) come out 나오다
12) bank with -은행과 거래하다
13) pick up -을 뽑다
14) a number ticket 번호 대기표

15) open an account 계좌를 개설하다
16) cash a check 수표를 현금으로 바꾸다
17) an identification 신분증
18) endorse the check 수표에 이서하다
19) denominations 액권
20) plastic money 신용카드 (= a credit card)
21) put a stop 지불정지를 하다
22) lost checks 분실수표
23) the exchange rate 환율
24) the interest rates 이율
25) per annum 1년에
26) a rubber check 부도수표 (= a bounced check)
27) deposit -을 예금하다
28) a deposit/withdrawal slip 입금/인출 전표
29) automatically transfer -을 자동이체하다
30) have - electronically wired -을 계좌이체하다

03 Key Expressions & Application Dialogues

1) A: Is there an ATM around here?
B: Not that I know of.

2) Teller : What's your PIN number?
Customer : Five-three-nine-six.

3) A: How do I go about using this ATM?
B: First, insert your cash card into the machine.
Second, select the type of service.
Third, enter your PIN number.
Fourth, enter the amount you wish to withdraw.
And lastly, take out the statement, and the money will come out.

4) A: Who are you banking with?
B: I'm banking with KB Star.

5) A: Do you have an account with us?
B: No. I'd like to open an account with this bank.

6) A: Excuse me, I'm here to update my bankbook.
B: Please pick up/take a number ticket and wait. It's over there.

7) A: I'd like to cash this check, please.
B: Do you have any identification with you?

8) A: I'd like to cash this traveler's check, please.
B: Have you endorsed the check?

9) A: Can you break a 100-dollar bill?
B: Sure. How would you like your money?

10) A: What denominations would you like?
B: I'd like eight tens and twenty singles.

11) A: Do you carry plastic money?
B: Yes. I have my Visa card.

12) A: May I help you, ma'am?
B: Yes. I'd like to put a stop on my lost checks.

13) A: What's the exchange rate today?
B: The current exchange rate is 1,304 won to the dollar.

14) A: What are your interest rates?
B: You'll get 5.6% interest per annum.

15) What is the exchange rate for US dollars to Korean won?

16) I'd like to change US dollars into pounds, please.

17) I'd like my electricity bill paid directly from my account.

18) I received a rubber check from a customer.

19) The check is bounced.

20) I'd like to deposit some money into my bank account.

21) I'd like to withdraw 100,000 won from my bank account.

22) Could you fill out a deposit/withdrawal slip?

23) My company automatically transfers my salary to this bank.

24) My salary is paid directly into my bank account.

25) I'd like to have 300,000 won (electronically) wired to Mary's account.

04 Review : *Fill in the blanks*

1. are with you who banking
   (어느 은행과 거래하고 계십니까?)
   ____________________________?

2. ATM here is there an around
   (이 근처에 현금자동지급기가 있어요?)
   ________________________________?

3. with account do us an have you
   (저희은행에 계좌를 가지고 계십니까?)
   ____________________________________?

4. bank in line time I spent much at this
   (나는 이 은행에서 줄을 서서 많은 시간을 보냈어요.)
   ____.

5. you have you identification do with any
   (신분증명할 것을 갖고 계십니까?)
   ____?

6. on a like stop my to checks put I'd lost
   (나의 분실수표에 대하여 지불정지를 하고 싶습니다.)
   ____.

7. rubber check customer I a received a from
   (한 손님에게서 부도수표를 받았어요.)
   ____.

8. open I'd bank account like to an with this
(이 은행에 계좌를 개설하고 싶습니다.)

____.

9. available the ATM isn't service at round-the-clock
(그 현금자동지급기는 24시간 서비스가 가능하지 않나요?)

____?

10. bank my salary transfers to my company this automatically
(저희 회사에서는 이 은행으로 제 봉급을 자동이체 시켜줍니다.)

____.

영어표현에 나타난 미국문화

The Great Sand Rush

해변백사장쇄도(海邊白沙場殺到)

미국의 서부개척시대에는 사람들이 부(富)를 축적하기 위하여 새로운 금광지대를 찾아 몰려들었다. 이를 Gold Rush(금광쇄도)라고 부르는데, 1849년에 있었던 미국 California 주에서의 금광쇄도(金鑛殺到)가 특히 유명하다. 근자에 와서 미국인들은 바다전망이 좋은 주택이나 콘도식 별장을 매입하려고 해변백사장근처로 몰려드는데, 이러한 현상은 1800년대 중반에 미국에서 있었던 Gold Rush를 연상시키기 때문에 the Great Sand Rush라고 부른다.

In relentless pursuit of an ocean view, millions of Americans have joined **the Great Sand Rush** in recent years, paying nosebleed prices for houses and condos on or near beaches. (멋진 바다경치를 무모하게 찾아 나서다보니, 수백만 명의 미국인들이 해변이나 해변근처에 있는 집과 콘도의 매입 비용으로 엄청난 금액을 지불하면서, 요사이 몇 년 사이에 (금광쇄도를 연상시키는) 해변백사장쇄도(海邊白沙場殺到)에 뛰어 들어왔다.)

Unit 10

Situational English

우체국 업무 관련표현

01 Conversation

[Did you enclose any letters?]

Clerk : How may I help you?
Client : I'd like to have this package sent by airmail, please.
Clerk : Where's it going?
Client : To Seoul, Korea.
Clerk : What does it contain?
Client : It contains books.
Clerk : **Did you enclose any letters?**
Client : No. It contains only books.
Clerk : OK. Please fill out this form. Do you want insurance on them?
Client : Yes, please.

02 Vocabulary

1) contain -을 포함하다
2) enclose -을 동봉하다
3) fill out -을 작성하다
4) insurance 보험
5) a package 소포 (= a parcel)
6) by airmail 비행기편으로 (= by air)
7) by surface mail 배편으로 (= by sea mail)
8) put something in the mail -을 우편으로 부치다
9) be supposed to -하도록 되어있다
10) seal -을 밀봉하다

11) cut the corner off 모서리를 잘라내다
12) rent a P.O. Box 우체국 사서함(P.O.B/post-office box)을 개설하다
13) just in case 만약의 경우를 대비해서
14) insure -에 보험을 들다
15) the return address 발신인/발송인 주소 (= the sender's address)
16) the zip code 우편 번호
17) be delivered 배달되다
18) stamps 우표 (= postage stamps)
19) snail mail 이메일(e-mail)에 비해 배달 속도가 느린 일반 우편
20) by registered mail 등기 우편으로
21) by special deliveries 속달 우편으로
22) door-to-door deliveries 택배
23) damaged 손상된
24) wrapping paper 포장지
25) tear 찢어지다
26) a string 끈
27) break 끊어지다
28) legibly 읽기 쉽게, 명료하게
29) in block letters 정자로 또박또박
30) by overnight mail 익일 배달 우편으로

03 Key Expressions & Application Dialogues

1) A: May I help you?
B: Yes, I'd like to send this package to Seoul.

2) A: How do you want to send it, by airmail or surface mail?
B: By airmail, please.

3) A: Did you enclose a letter?
B: No, I didn't. It's only books.

4) A: Are there any letters enclosed?
B: No. It contains only books.

5) A: Are there any letters in there?
B: No, there are only books in it.

6) A: The book hasn't arrived yet.
B: Are you sure, though? I put it in the mail a week ago.

7) A: You are not supposed to seal this package completely.
B: May I cut the corner off?

8) A: I'd like to rent a P.O. Box?
B: Would you like a small or big box?

9) A: Would you like to insure the parcel?
B: Yes, please. Just in case.

10) A: Is there anything I'm forgetting?
B: Yes. Please write the return address.
And you need to include the zip code.

11) A: When will this package be delivered?
B: It will take about four or five days.

12) A: How long will it take to get to Seoul?
B: It'll get there a week later.

13) A: Where can I get stamps?
B: Over there, at Window No. 3.

14) A: Snail mail takes long.
B: Right. That's why I prefer to use e-mail.

15) I'd like this letter sent by registered mail.

16) I'd like this package sent by special delivery.

17) We provide door-to-door deliveries.

18) The parcel arrived damaged in the mail.

19) This wrapping paper is too thin. It will tear.

20) This string is too weak, and it will break.
Use a stronger string.

21) This package isn't wrapped properly.
Please wrap it again and use stronger paper.

22) Write your name legibly in block letters.

23) Is there any way to check what happened to my parcel?

24) Write your address in the upper left-hand corner of the envelope.

25) You can send it by overnight mail.

04 Review : *Put the words in the correct order.*

1. the off may corner I cut
(모서리를 오려낼까요?)
________________________________.

2. ago put in a the mail week I it
(제가 일주일 전에 그것을 우편으로 부쳤어요.)
____.

3. am is forgetting there I anything
(내가 뭐 잊고 있는 것이라도 있나요?)
_______________________________________?

4. overnight it you send by mail can
(그것을 익일 배달 우편으로 보내시면 됩니다.)
____.

5. deliveries provide we door-to-door
(저희는 택배를 해드려요.)
____.

6. not this properly is wrapped package
(이 소포는 제대로 포장되지 않았어요.)
____.

7. package be will when this delivered
(이 소포는 언제까지 배달됩니까?)
____?

8. write letters your legibly in name block
(당신의 이름을 정자로 또박또박 읽기 쉽게 쓰세요.)

____.

9. airmail sent would to this I letter by like have
(나는 이 편지를 항공우편으로 부치고 싶습니다.)

____.

10. seal supposed are not to this you package completely
(이 소포를 완전히 밀봉하지 않도록 되어있습니다.)

____.

영어표현에 나타난 미국문화

Pack Rat Habit

(물건을 버리지 않고 모아두는 습관)

쓰던 물건이 아무리 낡아도 버리지 않고, 언젠가는 쓸모가 있을 것이라는 생각에서 집안 구석구석에 보관해두는 습관을 가리켜 pack rat habit이라고 한다. pack rat은 북미지역에 서식하는 큰 쥐의 일종으로서, 물건을 보면 닥치는 대로 물어다가 굴속에 옮겨 모아두는 습성이 있다는 것에서 유래한 표현이다. 별로 오래 사용하지도 않아 아직은 쓸 만한 물건을 버리는 습관(throw-away habit)도 좋지 않지만, 낡은 물건을 모아두는 습관도 역시 집안을 정리하지 않고 여기저기에 정신없이 늘어놓아 집안 구석구석을 너저분하게 만드는 습관(clutter habit)과 더불어 고쳐야할 습관이다.

Not everyone is born with **the neatness gene**, but try to change your **pack rat habit**. Maintain better files by **kicking the clutter habit** for good.
(모든 사람들이 깔끔하게 정리하는 **성품의 인자(因子)**를 지니고 태어나지는 않지만, 물건을 버리지 않고 모아두는 습관을 바꿔보세요. **여기저기 늘어놓는 습관**을 아주 **버려**서 더 멋진 서류철을 유지하세요.)

Situational English

Unit 11

교통 및 운전 관련표현

01 Conversation

[Is it a long ride to the hotel?]

Cabman : Where to, sir?
Traveler : I want to go to the Walker Hill Hotel.
Cabman : OK. Hop in.
Traveler : **Is it a long ride to the hotel?**
Cabman : Yes. It will take about half an hour.
There's always a lot of traffic at this time of the day.
Traveler : Wow, the traffic during the rush hour is at a crawl.
Cabman : Right. Cars are bumper to bumper on the streets.
It's backed up for miles.
Traveler : The meter keeps going up even when we are stuck in a gridlock.
Are we there yet?
Cabman : We're almost there.

02 Vocabulary

1) be a long ride 장시간 차를 타고 가다
2) at a crawl 기듯이 가는 (= at a snail's pace)
3) bumper to bumper 교통체증으로 꽉 차서 서있는
4) be backed up 밀리다, 정체되다
5) be stuck in a gridlock 교통체증에 걸리다
6) bend the rule 편의대로 규정을 살짝 어기다

7) be stuck on red 신호등에 빨간 불이 들어 온 상태로 고장 나다
8) a rule bender 편의대로 규정을 살짝 어기는 사람
9) slow down 속력을 낮추다
10) a speed trap 속도 측정 장치 (= a speed camera / a speed gun / a radar gun)
11) up ahead 앞쪽에
12) move at a snail's pace 천천히 움직이다
13) a sobriety checkpoint 음주 운전 검문소 (= a DUI checkpoint)
14) blow into -에 입김을 불어넣다, -을 불다
15) the breathalyzer 음주 측정기
16) the BAC (= the blood alcohol concentration) 혈중 알코올 농도
17) DUI (= driving under the influence) 음주 운전
(= DWI; driving while intoxicated)
18) a speed bump 과속 방지턱
19) drag on the bottom 바닥이 끌리다
20) run the red light 빨간 신호등을 무시하고 달리다
21) a ticket 교통위반 딱지(= a traffic ticket/citation)
22) give somebody a break -를 한번 눈감아 주다, -를 봐 넘겨주다
23) the fuel gauge 연료 계기판
24) slam on -을 급히 밟다
25) run on propane fuel LPG 가스로 달리다 (= run on propane)
26) secure -을 확실하게 하다
27) road holding 노면 접지성
28) tailgate -를 바짝 따라 붙어 운전하다
29) the slow traffic turnout 저속 차량 레인
30) the ice scraper 성에 제거기

03 Key Expressions & Application Dialogues

1) A: You are bending the traffic rules.
Wait for the traffic light to change.
B: No way. It's stuck on red. I'm not a rule bender.

2) A: Slow down. There's a speed trap up ahead.
B: Thanks.

3) A: I'm wondering why cars are moving at a snail's pace?
B: There's a sobriety checkpoint up ahead.

4) A: Excuse me, sir. Blow into this breathalyzer, please.
B: I'm sorry, but your BAC is a DUI case.

5) A: Pick up your feet. There's a speed bump.
B: Whoops! It drags on the bottom.

6) A: You were speeding, ma'am. May I see your driver's license?
B: Here you are.

7) A: You ran the red light. I'll have to give you a ticket.
B: I'm sorry, but can you give me a break this time?

8) A: Your fuel gauge is close to empty.
B: Really? I think I need to stop and gas up the tank.

9) A: Why were you late?
B: There was a car accident on my way to work.

10) A: Why were you so late?
B: I was caught in a traffic jam. Besides, there was a DUI checkpoint on my way here.

11) A: This snow tire has more bite on packed snow.
B: But don't slam on the brake.

12) A: Does this car run on gas or diesel?
B: It runs on propane fuel.

13) A: I see you put wide tires on your car.
B: Yes. They secure good road holding.

14) Here comes our bus. Please hop on.

15) Fill up the tank. Your fuel gauge is on empty.

16) My fuel gauge is on full.

17) I need a tune-up.

18) I need to jump-start my car

19) Traffic isn't moving. Sometimes there's only a stop-and-go.

20) You can drop me off anywhere along the way.

21) The car behind me is tailgating me.

22) Use the slow traffic turnout.

23) Slow down. The driver won't let you into his lane.

24) The windshield is frosted all over. Use the ice scraper.

25) Put your lights on low beam when meeting another vehicle.

04 Review : *Put the words in the correct order.*

1. DUI case BAC your is a
(당신의 혈중 알코올 농도는 음주 운전에 해당합니다.)
_______________________________.

2. lights put low your on beam
(전조등을 하향으로 켜세요.)
__________________________________.

3. ride hotel it a to is the long
(호텔까지는 차를 오래 타고 가나요?)
___________________________________?

4. in was a traffic caught I jam
(저는 교통체증에 걸렸어요.)
____________________________________.

5. gas this run car on or does diesel
(이 차는 가솔린차예요, 아니면 경유차예요?)
____?

6. tailgating the me is me car behind
(내 뒤에 오는 차가 내 차에 바짝 따라 붙어 운전을 해요.)
____.

7. this break can give a time you me
(이번 한번만 봐주시면 안 되나요?)
____?

8. ahead there a up sobriety is checkpoint
(앞쪽에 음주 운전 검문소가 있어요.)

____.

9. way the anywhere me you drop can off along
(가다가 아무데나 저를 내려 주시면 됩니다.)

____.

10. my morning way work I a ticket on to this got speeding
(저는 오늘 아침 회사 오는 길에 속도위반 딱지 떼였어요.)

____.

영어표현에 나타난 미국문화

Northbound Lane and Southbound Lane

(상행선과 하행선)

우리나라에서는 상행선이라고 하지만 미국인들은 이 말을 upbound lane이라고 하지 않고 northbound lane이라고 하며, 하행선을 downbound lane이라고 하지 않고 southbound lane이라고 한다는 점에 유의해야한다. 한국인들은 북쪽과 남쪽을 상·하로, 그리고 동쪽과 서쪽을 좌·우로 지칭하지만 영미문화권에서는 방위를 나타내는 north, south, east, and west의 사용을 고집한다. 아울러, 우리는 동서남북이라고 말하지만 영어로는 north, south, east, and west라고 한다.

To get from my home in Cheonan to Seoul, I must squeeze into **northbound traffic** on Route 31.
(천안에 있는 우리 집에서 서울에 가려면, 나는 31번 국도에서 **상행선 차량통행**에 끼어들어가야 한다.)

항공여행 관련표현

01 Conversation

[May I see your ticket and passport, please?]

Clerk : May I help you, sir?
Passenger : Yes, please.
Clerk : **May I see your ticket and passport, please?**
Passenger : Here you go.
Clerk : Do you have a seating preference?
Passenger : An aisle seat, please.
Clerk : And do you have any luggage to check in?
Passenger : Yes, I have one bag.
Clerk : Could you put that on the scale, please?
Passenger : Sure.
Clerk : All right, sir. Here's your boarding pass. Your seat number is 7A. It's Gate 32, boarding at 2:20. Have a good flight!
Passenger : Thank you.

02 Vocabulary

1) a passport 여권
2) a seating preference 선호하는 좌석
3) an aisle seat 통로 좌석
4) luggage 수하물

5) check in 체크인 하다, 탑승 수속을 하다
6) the scale 저울
7) a boarding pass 탑승권
8) the gate 탑승구 (= the boarding gate)
9) a breakfast flight 아침이 제공되는 비행기
10) a lunch flight 점심이 제공되는 비행기
11) a party of three 일행이 세 사람
12) open-ended 시간이 제한되어 있지 않은
13) the departure time 출발 시각
14) the purpose 목적
15) for sightseeing 관광하러 (= on vacation / for pleasure)
16) declare -을 신고하다
17) prohibited items 소지 금지된 물품들
18) open up -을 열어서 보여주다
19) prior to -전에 (= before / ahead of)
20) security screening 보안 검사
21) a tourist brochure 관광 안내 책자
22) a frequent flyer mileage card 상용 이용자 마일리지 카드
23) not allowed 허용이 되지 않는 (= prohibited)
24) pills 알약
25) sickness 멀미
26) recline -을 뒤로 젖히다
27) put forward -을 앞으로 젖히다/일으켜 주다
28) make a reservation 예약하다
29) the waiting list 대기자 명단
30) the baggage claim 수하물 찾는 곳

03 Key Expressions & Application Dialogues

1) A: Is this a breakfast flight?
B: No, sir. This is a lunch flight.

2) A: Good morning. Would you like to check in now?
B: Yes, we're a party of three and we'd like to sit together.

3) A: How much luggage do you want to check in?
B: Two bags, please.

4) A: Can I leave my tickets open-ended?
B: Certainly, sir.

5) A: Where's the boarding gate?
B: Gate 32.

6) A: What's the departure time?
B: It's 11:30.

7) A: What's the arrival time?
B: 10:30. It's just one hour away.

8) A: Stewardess, may I have a blanket?
B: Certainly, sir. Wait a moment, please.

9) A: What would you like to have, sir? Beef or chicken?
B: Chicken, please.

10) A: What's the purpose of your visit?
B: I'm here for sightseeing.

11) A: How long are you going to stay here?
B: About a week.

12) A: Do you have anything to declare?
B: No, I don't.

13) A: Do you have any prohibited items?
B: No, I don't.

14) A: Could you open up your suitcase for me, please?
B: Certainly.

15) A: Why should I be at the airport at least two hours prior to departure time?
B: Oh, it's for check-in and security screening.

16) A: Where can I have a city map and tourist brochure?
B: Oh, the tourist information center is right there.

17) I need a frequent flyer mileage card.

18) Smoking is not allowed on this flight.

19) Stewardess, would you give me some pills for sickness?

20) How do I get my seat to recline?

21) Excuse me. Could you put your seat forward?

22) I'd like to make a reservation for a flight to Seoul.

23) Could you put my name on the waiting list?

24) When is our plane scheduled to arrive in Seoul?

25) Let's pick up our luggage from the baggage claim.

04 Review : *Put the words in the correct order.*

1. declare do anything you have to
(신고할 물품이 있으십니까?)
________________________________?

2. seat could put forward you your
(당신의 좌석을 앞으로 일으켜주시겠어요?)
________________________________?

3. the your is purpose of visit what
(당신의 방문 목적은 무엇인가요?)
________________________________?

4. have preference do a seating you
(선호하는 좌석이 있습니까?)
________________________________?

5. flyer card I a frequent mileage need
(나는 마일리지카드가 필요합니다.)
________________________________.

6. luggage do check you any to in have
(부칠 짐이 있으세요?)
________________________________?

7. check-in what is your the time for flight?
(당신의 비행기 편은 탑승수속시간이 언제입니까?)
________________________________?

8. for would sickness you give some pills me
(멀미약 좀 주시겠어요?)
____?

9. waiting could put you my on the list name
(저의 이름을 대기자명단에 올릴 수 있나요?)
____?

10. pick baggage up our from let's the claim luggage
(수하물 찾는 곳에서 우리 짐을 찾읍시다.)
____.

영어표현에 나타난 미국문화

Doggie bag

(남은 음식 싸가는 봉지)

음식점에서 고기 같은 것을 구워먹다가 배가 불러 남기게 되는 음식을 집으로 포장해서 가지고 가는 일은 미국에서도 보편적인 관행처럼 받아들여진다. 이때 음식점에서 **Can I have a doggie bag, please? (남은 음식 좀 싸주세요!)**라는 표현을 쓰면 된다. 흔히 하기 좋은 말로, '우리 개에게 주려고 싸서 가져가는 봉지'라는 의미로 doggie bag이라는 명칭을 사용하지만 개보다는 오히려 사람이 먹는 일이 많은 것 같았다.

I make a doggie bag of an in-flight meal that seems edible and nutritious but is served at a time I'm not ready to eat. You know, the airsickness bag is a handy waterproof container.
(먹음직스러우면서 영양가가 있는데도 먹고 싶은 생각이 들지 않을 시간에 나오는 **기내식을 나는 비닐봉지에 싸가지고 와요**. 그런데 말이죠, 기내의 멀미용 봉투는 방수가 되는 간편한 용기이거든요.)

호텔투숙 관련표현

01 Conversation

[I'd like a room with a view of the city.]

Clerk : Can I help you, sir?
Traveler : Yes, I have a reservation.
Clerk : What name is it under?
Traveler : It's under Mr. John Kim.
Clerk : Let's see. Yes, you have a reservation for a double room with bath.
Traveler : **I'd like a room with a view of the city.**
Clerk : Very well, sir. Just a minute, please. We have a room commanding a good view of the city on the tenth floor.
Traveler : OK. I'll take it.

02 Vocabulary

1) have a reservation 예약이 되어 있다
2) a double room 2인용 객실
3) with bath 욕실이 딸린
4) with a view of the city 도시 경관이 보이는
5) commanding a good view 전망이 좋은
6) check in 호텔에 투숙하다
7) a single room 1인용 객실
8) facing south 남향의
9) a vacancy 빈방 (= a vacant room)
10) be filled up 예약이 다 차다
11) be all booked up 예약이 다 차다 (= be fully booked up)

12) the reservation desk 예약 데스크
13) get off 내리다
14) in an hour or so 한 시간 정도 후에
15) speed up -을 서둘러 하다
16) the arrival 도착
17) recommend -을 추천하다
18) browse -을 찾아보다
19) the Yellow Pages 업종별 전화번호부
20) return the key 열쇠를 반납하다
21) the front desk 호텔 프론트
22) check out 체크아웃 하다, 퇴실하다
23) make reservations 예약하다
24) far in advance 충분히 미리
25) lodging 숙박
26) fish-oriented menus 생선 요리 중심의 메뉴
27) have a "No Vacancy" sign up “빈방 없음” 간판을 켜 놓다
28) the rate 요금
29) charge 요금을 청구하다
30) walk-ins 예약을 하지 않고 오는 사람

03 Key Expressions & Application Dialogues

1) A: May I help you, ma'am?
B: Yes, I'd like to check in. I have a reservation.

2) A: What kind of room would you like, sir?
B: A single room with bath, please.

3) B: Would you like a single room or a double room?
A: A single room facing south, please.

4) A: Do you have any vacancies?
B: I'm sorry, sir. We are filled up.

4) A: Do you have any vacant rooms?
B: Sorry, we're all booked up.

5) A: Do you have any rooms available for tonight?
B: I'm sorry, but we have no vacancy.

6) A: Do you have a reservation?
B: No, but do you have a room available for tonight?

7) A: Is this the Hilton Hotel's reservation desk?
B: Yes. May I help you, ma'am?

8) A: I'm calling from Los Angeles International Airport.
I'd like to know if a single room is available for tonight.
B: I'm sorry, sir. We are fully booked up.

9) A: Could you tell me the best place to get off to reach the hotel?
B: Sure. Please get off at the City Market and take a taxi from there.
That's the quickest, best way.

10) A: I'm calling from the airport. I'll be there in an hour or so.
B: OK. We'll hold your room for you until 10 p.m.

11) A: I'll get there by 10 p.m.
B: Could you speed up your arrival, sir?

12) A: Could you recommend a hotel in this part of the city?
B: Well, why don't you browse the Yellow Pages?

13) A: How long is your stay here, sir?
B: Well, just one night.

14) A: Do I have to return the key when I check out?
B: Yes, to the front desk, please.

15) A: I'd like to check out. Here is my key.
B: All right, ma'am. Did you enjoy your stay with us?

16) A: Hello, I'm checking out. Here is the key.
B: We hope you had a good time here.

17) How many nights will you stay here?

18) How long are you going to stay with us?

19) Make reservations as far in advance as possible.
Lodging in this part of the city fills quickly.

20) This hotel restaurant offers fish-oriented menus.

21) That hotel has a "No Vacancy" sign up.

22) What's your rate for a single room?

23) How much do you charge for a double room?

24) Lotte Travel Agency recommended your hotel to me.

25) Walk-ins are welcome. We still have vacant rooms.

04 Review : *Fill in the blanks*

1. reservation you have do a
   (예약을 하고 오셨습니까?)
   ______________________________?

2. return have to the I key do
   (열쇠를 반납해야 합니까?)
   ______________________________?

3. hour or be in an so there I'll
   (한 시간 정도 후면 그곳에 도착 하겠습니다.)
   ______________________________.

4. single facing like a I'd room south.
   (남향의 1인용 객실을 주세요.)
   ______________________________.

5. no sorry we I'm have vacancy but
   (죄송하지만, 빈방이 없습니다.)
   ______________________________.

6. your for a what's double rate room
   (2인용 객실 요금이 얼마 입니까)
   ______________________________?

7. view I'd a with a of like the city room
   (도시 경관이 보이는 방을 주세요.)
   ______________________________.

8. browse why you the Yellow don't Pages
(업종별 전화번호부를 찾아보시는 게 어때요?)

____?

9. are long with going to how stay us you
(저희 호텔에서는 얼마나 오래 머무르실 겁니까?)

____?

10. rooms you any available for do have tonight?
(오늘 밤에 투숙할 수 있는 방이 있습니까?)

____?

영어표현에 나타난 미국문화

(As) phony as the Arnold Schwarzenegger DVD

(진품이 아니고, 완전히 가짜인)

미국인들은 어떤 물건이 가짜라는 것을 강조할 때 phony as a three-dollar bill 이라고 말한다. 미화는 지폐의 액면가(denominations)가 $1, $5, $10, $20, $50, $100 등으로 되어 있으나, $3 짜리지폐는 없기 때문에 3달러만큼 가짜라고 하면, 아주 가짜라는 말이 된다. 아놀드 슈워제네거는 영화배우를 지냈고 현재는 미국 캘리포니아 주지사인데, 그가 DVD를 냈을 리가 없으니까 아놀드 슈워제네거 DVD만큼 가짜라고 하면, 이 표현 역시 가짜라는 것을 강조하는—미국현지사정을 반영한—시사성표현(時事性表現)이 된다.

Why don't you take time out for a visit to still bargain-priced Beijing? But be careful that most of the collector's items in Beijing may be just as phony **as the Arnold Schwarzenegger DVD**.
(아직도 염가(廉價)인 북경을 방문하기 위하여 시간을 좀 내세요. 하지만 북경에서 명품(名品)들 중의 대부분은 (아놀드 슈워제네거 DVD처럼) **아주 가짜**일 수도 있다는 것을 주의하세요.)

Situational English

Unit 14

렌터카 관련표현

01 Conversation

[I'd like to rent a car.]

Traveler : Hello. **I'd like to rent a car.**
Rental : Do you have an international driver's license?
Traveler : Yes, Here you are.
Rental : OK. What type of car are you interested in?
Traveler : I'd like a full-size car.
Do you have a Mercedes Benz available?
Rental : Certainly. Just a minute, sir. Here's a list of charges.
Insurance and a tankful of gas are included.
Traveler : OK. I'll take it.
Rental : Please fill out this form. And here are your keys.
Let me show you to your car.

02 Vocabulary

1) an international driver's license 국제운전면허증 (= an international driving permit)
2) a full-size car 대형 승용차
3) a list of charges 요금 목록
4) insurance 보험
5) a tankful of gas 가득 채운 연료
6) the rent-a-car booth 자동차를 대여 하는 곳
7) a medium-size car 중형 승용차
8) drop-off charges 자동차를 대여한 곳이 아닌 다른 곳에다 차를 반납할 때 지불해야 하는 비용
9) check under the hood 자동차 앞쪽 보닛을 열어 엔진오일 등을 점검하다

10) fill up -을 가득 채우다 (= top off)
11) a tow-away zone 견인 지역
12) pull up on the shoulder 차를 노견에 세우다
13) a penalty for extended use 초과 사용에 따른 수수료 (= a late fee)
14) good gas mileage 좋은 연비
15) a gas sipper 연료를 적게 먹는 차
16) need a ride 자동차 편승이/교통편이 필요하다 (= need a lift)
17) get in 타다 (= jump/hop in)
18) go one's way -와 같은 방향으로 가다
19) give someone a ride -를 태워주다 (= give someone a lift)
20) ride shotgun 자동차 앞자리 조수석에 타다
21) drive on the job 직업으로 운전하다
22) have a flat tire 자동차 타이어가 펑크 나다
23) look low 자동차에 바람이 빠진 것 같다
24) back-in parking 후면 주차
25) head-in parking 전면 주차
26) an emergency roadside kit 차량용 비상 물품함
27) pop the trunk 자동차 트렁크를 열다
28) sit behind the wheel 운전하다 (= drive)
29) parallel-park 병렬로/나란히 주차 하다
30) validate one's parking ticket -에게 주차 확인증을 찍어주다

03 Key Expressions & Application Dialogues

1) A: Excuse me. Where's the rent-a-car booth?
B: You can see it at the far end of the airport lobby.

2) A: What type of car are you interested in?
B: I'd like a medium-size car.

3) A: When it comes to returning the car, can I leave it somewhere else?
B: No. Cars have to be returned to the rental station.

4) A: Could I rent it one way?
B: Sure, but you have to pay drop-off charges.

5) A: Do I have to pay for oil as well?
B: No. The car is all checked under the hood and oil is put in before it goes out.

6) A: Did you fill up the tank with gas?
B: Yes. I topped it off.

7) A: Is this a tow-away zone?
B: Yes. Pull up on the shoulder.

8) A: I was supposed to return this car yesterday.
B: There's a penalty for extended use.
You'll have to pay a late fee.

10) A: Your car gets good gas mileage.
B: Yes. I think it's a gas sipper.

11) A: Do you need a ride?
B: Thank you. Can I get in?

12) A: Are you going my way?
B: Sure. Jump in.

13) A: I'm going your way. Can you give me a ride?
B: Okay. Hop in.

14) A: Thank you for the ride. I'll ride shotgun.
B: Your door didn't shut.

15) Do you drive on the job?

16) Would you go for a ride?

17) I have a flat tire.

18) Your left front tire looks a little low.

19) I'd like to rent a car one way.
Is there a drop-off charge?

20) No back-in parking. Head-in parking is encouraged here.

21) May I see your driver's license, please?

22) Can you use your emergency roadside kit? Please pop the trunk.

23) Do not drink and drive. (= Don't sit behind the wheel while drunk.)

24) Parallel-park close to the curb.

25) Could you validate my parking ticket?

04 Review : *Fill in the blanks*

1. tow-away is a zone this
(여기는 견인지역입니다.)
_______________________________.

2. give you me a can ride
(저 좀 태워주시겠어요?)
_______________________________?

3. your me you to car let show
(제가 차 있는데 까지 안내해 드리겠습니다.)
_______________________________________.

4. gets your gas car good mileage
(당신 차는 연비가 좋군요.)
____.

5. driver's may see your I license
(운전면허증 좀 보여 주시겠습니까?)
____?

6. you up the tank did with gas fill
(자동차 연료 탱크는 가득 채웠나요?)
____?

7. is here parking encouraged head-in
(이곳에서는 전면 주차를 권장합니다.)
____.

8. validate could ticket you my parking
(주차 확인증 좀 찍어 주시겠어요?)
______________________________________?

9. tire left low front looks a your little
(당신의 왼쪽 앞 타이어에 바람이 좀 빠진 것 같아요.)
______________________________________.

10. car I was return to this yesterday supposed
(저는 이 차를 어제 반납하기로 되어 있었습니다.)
______________________________________.

영어표현에 나타난 미국문화

Since Noah was a boy.

(아주 오래 전부터)

영어를 영어답게 하려면 미국인들이 현재 잘 쓰는 비유표현을 많이 알아두고 그들이 말하는 대로 모방해야한다. 특히, 고정되어있는 기존의 관용표현보다는 현대의 시사성을 가미한 비유표현을 자연스럽게 사용하기가 훨씬 어렵다. 마치 미국인이 아무리 한국말을 잘한다고 하더라도 "게으른 그가 부자가 된다면 **내 손가락에 장을 지지겠다.**"라는 토속적인 말이나, "김 교수는 **박세리나 최경주를 빰칠 정도로** 골프를 잘 친다."라는 시사성이 곁들여진 말을 한국어로 거침없이 할 수 없는 것과 마찬가지이다.

His car **looks like it has been on the road since Noah was a boy**.
(그의 차는 **오래전부터 몰고 다닌 것 같이 낡아 보여요.**)

외관상으로 차가 녹슬고 너무 낡아빠진 것을 보면서, "당신 차는 노아의 어린 시절부터 도로를 주행해온 것처럼 보여요."라고 말하면 관용표현이 아니면서도 누구에게나 쉽게 이해가 되는 멋진 영어표현이 될 것이다.

정답 및 해설

Answer Key for 04 Review

Unit 00

1. What	2. Where	3. in	4. no	5. take
6. rides	7. chickens	8. There are	9. work	10. horse

Unit 01

1. Don't leave the TV on.
   (TV를 켜둔 채로 자리를 비우지 마세요.)
2. I'd give it two thumbs up.
   (나는 거기에 최고 점수를 주겠어요.)
3. Do you have a green thumb?
   (당신은 원예 솜씨가 있으세요?)
4. I do thirty sit-ups every day.
   (나는 매일 윗몸일으키기를 30번씩 합니다.)
5. Asan is a blind spot for AFKN.
   (아산은 AFKN 난시청지역입니다.)
6. The electric bill is really out of sight.
   (전기료가 터무니없이 많이 나와요.)
7. I'll have to get rid of my love handles.
   (나는 허릿살을 제거해야 해요.)
8. What do you usually do in your free time?
   (여가시간에는 대개 뭐하세요?)
9. Who in your family gets to hold the remote control?
   (당신의 집에서는 리모컨(채널) 주도권을 누가 갖고 있어요?)
10. The 9:00 p.m. news show enjoys the highest audience rating.
    (그 9시 뉴스 프로그램은 최고의 시청률을 자랑합니다.)

Unit 02

1. I'm a real movie buff.
   (저는 영화광이에요.)
2. I'm a big fan of Cho Yongpil.
   (저는 조용필의 열렬한 팬이에요.)

3. There are no more seats available.
   (가능한 좌석이 없습니다.)
4. Let's get a bite to eat at the KFC.
   (KFC에서 간단히 요기합시다.)
5. How often do you go to the movies?
   (영화는 얼마나 자주 보러 가세요?)
6. Would you like to catch a flick tonight?
   (오늘밤에 영화나 한편 볼까요?)
7. We'd like seats way back in the corner.
   (아주 뒤쪽 구석자리로 주세요.)
8. Do you have any particular movie in mind?
   (특별히 마음에 둔 영화가 있습니까?)
9. Let's get a Coke and a popcorn at the kiosk.
   (매점에서 코카콜라와 팝콘을 사도록 합시다.)
10. That show is a far cry from the original story.
    (그 영화는 원작과는 거리가 멀어요.)

Unit 03

1. Is he gone for the day?
   (그분은 아주 퇴근하셨나요?)
2. My cellphone is out of range.
   (여기는 핸드폰이 안 터지는 지역이에요.)
3. Let your fingers do the walking.
   (갈 것 없이 전화로 하세요.)
4. Set your cellphone to vibrate mode.
   (핸드폰을 진동모드로 해두세요.)
5. I'd like to speak to Mr. Smith, please.
   (김 선생님 좀 바꿔주세요.)
6. This cardphone is spitting my phone card.
   (이 공중전화는 내 전화카드를 밀어내고 있어요.)
7. I'm awfully sorry to call you at this late hour.
   (이렇게 늦은 시간에 전화를 드려서 죄송합니다.)
8. It's illegal to use a cellphone behind the wheel.
   (운전 중에 전화하는 것은 불법입니다.)

9. I'm going to sign up for the mobile phone service.
   (저는 이동전화 서비스에 가입할 작정이에요.)
10. Her phone number is not listed in the phone directory.
   (그녀의 전화번호는 전화번호부에 나와 있지 않아요.)

Unit 04

1. Duck under my umbrella.
   (내 우산 속으로 들어오세요.)
2. What's the weather like today?
   (오늘 날씨는 어떻습니까?)
3. I've got a frog in my throat.
   (나는 목이 잠겼어요.)
4. What's today's windchill factor?
   (오늘의 체감온도는 얼마예요?)
5. The bad cold hangs on and on.
   (그 심한 감기는 잘 떨어지지 않아요.)
6. It's frigid outside, so bundle up.
   (바깥 날씨가 매우 추우니까 옷을 두툼하게 입으세요.)
7. I got soaked to the skin in the rain.
   (나는 비에 흠뻑 젖었어요.)
8. Has the rainy spell come to an end yet?
   (이제 장마가 끝났나요?)
9. We're having perfect skiing weather today.
   (오늘은 스키타기에 아주 좋은 날씨예요.)
10. We are going to have sub-zero temperatures tomorrow.
   (내일은 영하의 날씨가 될 것입니다.)

Unit 05

1. How would you like your hair?
   (머리를 어떻게 해 드릴까요?)
2. Your haircut picks up your looks.
   (당신은 이발하니까 얼굴이 돋보이네요.)

3. Do you part your hair on the left?
(당신은 머리가르마를 왼쪽으로 타세요?)
4. Can you make layers in the back?
(머리 뒤쪽을 층지게 잘라 주시겠어요?)
5. What kind of perfume do you wear?
(당신은 어떤 향수를 쓰세요?)
6. Thin it out on the back of my head.
(머리 뒤쪽에 숱 좀 쳐주세요.)
7. Don't wear heavy makeup to the interview.
(인터뷰에는 화장을 짙게 하고 가지마세요.)
8. How do I look with these clip-on earrings?
(이 클립형 귀걸이가 저에게 잘 어울리나요?)
9. What beauty shop do you patronize the most?
(어느 미용실을 단골로 다니세요?)
10. She has long blonde hair flowing down her back.
(그녀는 등 뒤로 흘러내리는 긴 금발머리를 하고 있어요.)

Unit 06

1. Would you like to try it on?
(그것을 한번 입어 보실래요?)
2. It is a little too tight for me.
(그것은 내가 입기에 좀 끼어요.)
3. I'd like a refund on this shirt.
(이 셔츠를 환불받고 싶습니다.)
4. We strictly go by the price tag.
(저희가게에서는 엄격히 정찰제로 합니다.)
5. Do you have this in a larger size?
(이거 더 큰 사이즈로 있어요?)
6. When will it be ready for a fitting?
(언제 쯤 가봉이 됩니까?)
7. What price range do you have in mind?
(얼마 정도의 가격을 생각하고 계세요?)
8. Come in and treat yourself to a browse.
(들어와서 편히 구경하세요.)

9. Don't you think this jacket is too showy?
(이 재킷이 너무 화려한 것 같지 않아요?)
10. I am going clothes shopping in Myoungdong.
(나는 명동으로 의류 쇼핑하러 가고 있어요.)

Unit 07

1. The color may run if washed.
(물빨래를 하면 색깔이 바랠지도 모릅니다.)
2. I'm here to pick up my laundry.
(세탁물 맡긴 것을 찾으러 왔습니다.)
3. Are you going to do the laundry?
(빨래하시려는 거예요?)
4. This coffee stain won't come off.
(이 커피얼룩은 잘 빠지지 않아요.)
5. My jeans are ripped at the seams.
(제 데님바지의 솔기가 터졌어요.)
6. This material picks up a lot of dirt.
(이 재질은 먼지가 많이 붙어요.)
7. There's a laundromat in this building.
(이 건물에 동전세탁소가 하나 있어요.)
8. I'd like to have this suit dry-cleaned.
(이 정장을 드라이클리닝해주세요.)
9. I'd like it delivered to my apartment.
(제 아파트까지 배달해 주시면 좋겠습니다.)
10. We'll do our best to get the stain out.
(나는 최선을 다해 그 얼룩을 빼겠습니다.)

Unit 08

1. Is there a landmark nearby?
(근처에 중요시설물이 있나요?)
2. You are on the wrong floor.
(층수를 잘못 찾아오셨어요.)

3. Let's use the overhead crosswalk.
(보행자용 육교를 이용합시다.)
4. How do I get to the post office?
(우체국에 가려면 어떻게 가야 하나요?)
5. Is this your first time in L.A.?
(L.A.는 이번이 처음이세요?)
6. Do you have transportation available?
(차 같은 교통편은 있어요?)
7. I have a good memory for directions.
(저는 길눈이 밝아요.)
8. Please check at the information desk.
(안내데스크에 확인하세요.)
9. Only sub-compact cars are allowed anlge parking at the curb.
(경차들만이 연도(沿道)에 개구리주차가 허용됩니다.)
10. We are not allowed to drive in a bus-only lane on Sundays.
(일요일에는 버스전용차선에서 달리면 안 됩니다.)

Unit 09

1. Who are you banking with?
(어느 은행과 거래하고 계십니까?)
2. Is there an ATM around here?
(이 근처에 현금자동지급기가 있어요?)
3. Do you have an account with us?
(저희은행에 계좌를 가지고 계십니까?)
4. I spent much time in line at this bank.
(나는 이 은행에서 줄을 서서 많은 시간을 보냈어요.)
5. Do you have any identification with you?
(신분증명할 것을 갖고 계십니까?)
6. I'd like to put a stop on my lost checks.
(나의 분실수표에 대하여 지불정지를 하고 싶습니다.)
7. I received a rubber check from a customer.
(한 손님에게서 부도수표를 받았어요.)
8. I'd like to open an account with this bank.
(이 은행에 계좌를 개설하고 싶습니다.)

9. Isn't round-the-clock service available at the ATM?
   (그 현금자동지급기는 24시간 서비스가 가능하지 않나요?)
10. My company automatically transfers my salary to this bank.
   (저희 회사에서는 이 은행으로 제 봉급을 자동이체 시켜줍니다.)

Unit 10

1. May I cut the corner off?
   (모서리를 오려낼까요?)
2. I put it in the mail a week ago.
   (제가 일주일 전에 그것을 우편으로 부쳤어요.)
3. Is there anything I'm forgetting?
   (내가 뭐 잊고 있는 것이라도 있나요?)
4. You can send it by overnight mail.
   (그것을 익일 배달 우편으로 보내시면 됩니다.)
5. We provide door-to-door deliveries.
   (저희는 택배를 해드려요.)
6. This package isn't wrapped properly.
   (이 소포는 제대로 포장되지 않았어요.)
7. When will this package be delivered?
   (이 소포는 언제까지 배달됩니까?)
8. Write your name legibly in block letters.
   (당신의 이름을 정자로 또박또박 읽기 쉽게 쓰세요.)
9. I'd like to have this letter sent by airmail.
   (나는 이 편지를 항공우편으로 부치고 싶습니다.)
10. You are not supposed to seal this package completely.
   (이 소포를 완전히 밀봉하지 않도록 되어있습니다.)

Unit 11

1. Your BAC is a DUI case.
   (당신의 혈중 알코올 농도는 음주 운전에 해당합니다.)
2. Put your lights on low beam.
   (전조등을 하향으로 켜세요.)

3. Is it a long ride to the hotel?
(호텔까지는 차를 오래 타고 가나요?)
4. I was caught in a traffic jam.
(저는 교통체증에 걸렸어요.)
5. Does this car run on gas or diesel?
(이 차는 가솔린차예요, 아니면 경유차예요?)
6. The car behind me is tailgating me.
(내 뒤에 오는 차가 내 차에 바짝 따라 붙어 운전을 해요.)
7. Can you give me a break this time?
(이번 한번만 봐주시면 안 되나요?)
8. There is a sobriety checkpoint up ahead.
(앞쪽에 음주 운전 검문소가 있어요.)
9. You can drop me off anywhere along the way.
(가다가 아무데나 저를 내려 주시면 됩니다.)
10. I got a speeding ticket on my way to work this morning.
(저는 오늘 아침 회사 오는 길에 속도위반 딱지 떼였어요.)

Unit 12

1. Do you have anything to declare?
(신고할 물품이 있으십니까?)
2. Could you put your seat forward?
(당신의 좌석을 앞으로 일으켜주시겠어요?)
3. What's the purpose of your visit?
(당신의 방문 목적은 무엇인가요?)
4. Do you have a seating preference?
(선호하는 좌석이 있습니까?)
5. I need a frequent flyer mileage card.
(나는 마일리지카드가 필요합니다.)
6. Do you have any luggage to check in?
(부칠 짐이 있으세요?)
7. What's the check-in time for your flight?
(당신의 비행기 편은 탑승수속시간이 언제입니까?)
8. Would you give me some pills for sickness?
(멀미약 좀 주시겠어요?)

9. Could you put my name on the waiting list?
(저의 이름을 대기자명단에 올릴 수 있나요?)
10. Let's pick up our luggage from the baggage claim.
(수하물 찾는 곳에서 우리 짐을 찾읍시다.)

Unit 13

1. Do you have a reservation?
(예약을 하고 오셨습니까?)
2. Do I have to return the key?
(열쇠를 반납해야 합니까?)
3. I'll be there in an hour or so.
(한 시간 정도 후면 그곳에 도착 하겠습니다.)
4. I'd like a single room facing south.
(남향의 1인용 객실을 주세요.)
5. I'm sorry, but we have no vacancy.
(죄송하지만, 빈방이 없습니다.)
6. What's your rate for a double room?
(2인용 객실 요금이 얼마 입니까?)
7. I'd like a room with a view of the city.
(도시 경관이 보이는 방을 주세요.)
8. Why don't you browse the Yellow Pages?
(업종별 전화번호부를 찾아보시는 게 어때요?)
9. How long are you going to stay with us?
(저희 호텔에서는 얼마나 오래 머무르실 겁니까?)
10. Do you have any rooms available for tonight?
(오늘 밤에 투숙할 수 있는 방이 있습니까?)

Unit 14

1. This is a tow-away zone.
(여기는 견인지역입니다.)
2. Can you give me a ride?
(저 좀 태워주시겠어요?)

3. Let me show you to your car.
(제가 차 있는데 까지 안내해 드리겠습니다.)
4. Your car gets good gas mileage.
(당신 차는 연비가 좋군요.)
5. May I see your driver's license?
(운전면허증 좀 보여 주시겠습니까?)
6. Did you fill up the tank with gas?
(자동차 연료 탱크는 가득 채웠나요?)
7. Head-in parking is encouraged here.
(이곳에서는 전면 주차를 권장합니다.)
8. Could you validate my parking ticket?
(주차 확인증 좀 찍어 주시겠어요?)
9. Your left front tire looks a little low.
(당신의 왼쪽 앞 타이어에 바람이 좀 빠진 것 같다.)
10. I was supposed to return this car yesterday.
(저는 이 차를 어제 반납하기로 되어 있었습니다.)

부 록

Appendix

1. Idiomatic Expressions

1.1 Colloquial Idioms

She has an ear for music. (= She knows a lot about music.)
Your eyes are bigger than your stomach. (= You're greedy for food.)
He got up on the wrong side of the bed. (= He woke up in a bad mood.)
He kicked the bucket. (= He died.)
I feel under the weather today. (= I'm not in very good health today.)
The ball is in your court.
(= It's up to you to make the next decision. / It depends on you.)
He's in hot water. (= He's in trouble.)
It's a hot potato. (= It's a difficult problem.)
She's a shrinking violet. (= She is very shy and modest.)
He threw in the towel. (= He gave up.)
We're on the same wavelength. (= We're having similar opinions or tastes.)
He was born with a silver spoon in his mouth.
(= He was born into a rich family.)
I'm completely snowed under. (= I'm very, very busy.)
I'm all thumbs. (= I'm not good at it.)
I'm all ears. (= I'm eager to hear what you have to say.)
Break a leg! (= Good luck!)
It's on the back burner. (= It is being given low priority.)
He's a backseat driver.
(= He's an annoying person who is fond of giving advice to the person performing a task or doing something.)
He's a wet blanket.
(= He's a dull, boring person who spoils other people's happiness.)
I'm having a bad hair day today.
(= Things are not going my way today.)
Call a spade a spade. (= Let's be frank and honest.)
He's beating around the bush. (= He's not saying clearly what he means.)
He is a five-finger discounter. (= He is a shoplifter.)

1.2 Proverbial Idioms

Two heads are better than one.
(= Two people working together can solve a problem quicker and better than a person working alone.)
Too many cooks spoil the broth.
(= Too many people trying to take care of something can ruin it.)
Beauty lies in the eye of the beholder.
(= What seems ordinary or ugly to one person might seem beautiful to another.)
It's a drop in the bucket. (= It's practically nothing.)
It's a pie in the sky. (= It's an unrealistically Utopian plan or project.)
It's no use crying over spilt milk.
(= Don't grieve about having done something that cannot be undone.)
The pot calls the kettle black.
(= It's like criticizing other people without looking at your own faults first.)
Speak of the devil.
(= A reference to someone who appears unexpectedly while being talked about.)
The icing on the cake.
(= Something wonderful at the end of something good.)
It never rains but it pours.
(= Troublesome situations always seem to happen all at once.)
An apple a day keeps the doctor away.
(= Eating an apple everyday helps a person to stay healthy.)
Absence makes the heart grow fonder.
(= People often feel more affectionate toward each other when they are apart.)
Don't bite off more than you can chew. (= Don't be overconfident.)
Beggars can't be choosers.
(= When a person has nothing, he or she must accept whatever help is offered.)
All work and no play makes Jack a dull boy.
(= A person who spends all his time working will be a dull and uninteresting companion.)

1.3 Animal Idioms

(1) Cat Idioms

Don't let the cat out of the bag.
(= Don't spill the beans. / Keep it under your hat. / Don't tell the secret.)
The cat is out of the bag. (= The secret is already known.)
A cat has nine lives. (= A cat has a long life.)
It's raining cats and dogs. (= It's raining heavily.)
Care killed the cat. (= Care is dangerous.)
Curiosity killed the cat. (= Curiosity is dangerous.)
A scalded cat fears cold water.
(= A person who has had experience will shy away from certain things.)
Has the cat got your tongue? (= Why are you so silent?)
This food is enough to make a cat speak. (= This food is delicious.)
This is enough to make a cat laugh. (= This is very funny.)
That's the cat's meow/pajamas. (= That's great.)
When the cat's away, the mice will play.
(= Some people misbehave when they are not being watched.)
There's no room to swing a cat in his study.
(= There is not a lot of space in his study.)
A cat may look at a king.
(= No one is so important that an ordinary person cannot look at them.)
He's a fat cat. (= He's a successful businessman, with lots of money.)
He's a cat's paw.
(= He's an agent who carries out nefarious deeds for another.)
He's putting the cat among the pigeons. (= He's stirring up trouble.)
He's playing a cat and mouse game with me.
(= He's confusing me intentionally. / He's deceiving me.)
He is like a cat on hot bricks/on a hot tin roof. (= He's restless.)
He looks like the cat that swallowed/ate the canary.
(= He looks very satisfied.)
All cats appear grey in the dark.
(= Under certain conditions, we all appear the same.)
He's wearing a grin like a Cheshire cat.
(= He's smiling widely, showing all his teeth.)
They're fighting like Kilkenny cats. (= They're fighting fiercely.)

(2) Dog Idioms

He is in the dog house. (= He is in disgrace/trouble.)
He is under the black dog. (= He is blue.)
He is a dog in the manger. (= He is an ill-natured person.)
Let sleeping dogs lie. (= Don't make trouble when all is calm.)
Love me, love my dog.
(= If you love someone, you should accept everything and everyone that person loves.)
Every dog has his/its day. (= Everyone can be lucky.)
He works like a dog. (= He works very hard.)
If you lie down with dogs, you will get up with fleas.
(= If you associate with bad people, you will acquire their faults.)
His house has gone to the dogs. (= His house has become run-down.)
At open doors dogs come in. (= Opportunity makes a thief.)
You can't teach an old dog new tricks.
(= It's almost impossible for an elderly person to adopt a new routine.)
Barking dogs seldom bite.
(= People who threaten others usually do not harm them.)
If the old dog barks, he gives counsel.
(= If you wish good advice, consult an old man.)
Every dog is a lion at home. (= Every man is a king in his own home.)
He's a dead dog. (= He's nothing.)
Every dog is valiant at his own door.
(= Every man is a king in his own home.)
Hungry dogs will eat dirty puddings. (= Hunger is the best sauce.)

(3) Horse Idioms

He eats like a horse. (= He eats a lot of food. / He's a heavy eater.)
Don't look a gift horse in the mouth.
(= Don't assess the value of the gift that you have received.)
I've got a charley horse. (= I have a cramp in my legs.)
Get off your high horse. (= Come on, you are no better than anyone else.)
It's too late to shut the stable door after the horse has bolted.
(= It is easy to be wise after the event. Take appropriate precautions.)
A horse may stumble that has four legs.
(= Even Homer sometimes nods. Even the greatest make mistakes.)

I got it from the horse's mouth. (= I heard it from the highest authority.)
Don't change horses in midstream. (= Stick to your first plan.)
Don't put the cart before the horse.
(= First things first. Don't do things in the wrong order.)
Hungry horses make a clean manger. (= Hunger is the best sauce.)
A horse that will not carry a saddle must have no oats.
(= No pain, no gain. If you don't work, you cannot eat.)
This is a horse of a different color. (= This is a quite a different matter.)
If an ass a traveling, he'll not come home a horse.
(= Once a fool, always a fool.)
When the coach leaves the gym, he always horses around.
(= When the coach leaves the gym, he always aimlessly plays around.)

(4) Bird Idioms

A little bird told me. (= Someone told me. / I heard it through the grape vine.)
She eats like a bird. (= She eats just a little food.)
Birds of a feather flock together.
(= Like-minded people associate together. / People of the same type seem to gather together.)
Fine feathers make fine birds.
(= A person can be important just by wearing fine clothes.)
A bird in the hand is worth two in the bush.
(= Something you already have is better than something you might get.)
It's for the birds. (= It's uninteresting and meaningless.)
I'm an early bird. (= I get up early in the morning. I'm an early riser.)
The early bird catches the worm.
(= The person who gets up early to work will be successful.)
Kill two birds with one stone. (= Fulfil two purposes with one action.)

(5) Chicken Idioms

He runs around like a chicken with its head cut off.
(= He goes from one place to another in a disorganized way.)
I go to bed with the chickens. (= I go to bed very early.)
Chickens come home to roost.
(= We cannot escape the consequences of our actions. /
One's ill words may come back to cause one trouble.)

He snatched it like a chicken on a June bug.
(= He snatched it very quickly.)
Don't count your chickens before they are hatched.
(= Don't assume that something will be successful before it is certain./
It is better to only rely on what is certain.)
The two boys are playing chicken.
(= The two boys are doing something dangerous in order to see who gets frightened first and stops doing it.)
There's a chicken in every pot. (= There's enough food for every family.)

(6) Other Animal Idioms

That cock won't fight. (= That will never happen.)
They live like fighting cocks. (= They enjoy best possible food.)
As the old cock crows, the young cock learns.
(= Children will copy every move their parents make. /
Children take after their parents. / Monkey see, monkey do.)
He's the cock of the walk.
(= He's a conceited, bossy person who dominates others.)
She behaves like a hen mother. (= She's very protective.)
She's as mad as a wet hen. (= She's very angry.)
He's a hen-pecked husband. (= His wife wears the pants in the family.)
Honest politicians are as scarce as hen's teeth.
(= Honest politicians are very scarce or nonexistent.)
I feel like a fish out of other. (= I feel uncomfortable.)
Fish and guests stink after three days.
(= A constant guest is never welcome.)
He drinks like a fish. (= He drinks too much alcoholic beverages.)
He's mute as a fish. (= He's silent.)
He's a big fish in a small pond.
(= He prefers respect within a small community.)
I have other fish to fry. (= I have other important things to do.)
He's a little fish in a big pond.
(= He's a lack-of-standing in a large community.)

There are plenty of other fish in the sea.
(= Don't be discouraged if you don't get the one you want—others are available.)
She took the bull by the horns.
(= She took decisive action in a different situation.)
To cast pearls before swine.
(= Don't give things to a person who doesn't know the value of them.)
I smell a rat. (= I feel that something is wrong.)
I'm on the pig's back. (= I'm very happy.)
What's good for the goose is good for the gander.
(= People should be treated equally, regardless of their gender.)
I have butterflies in my stomach (= I'm very nervous.)
I have a frog in my throat. (= My voice is hoarse.)
A leopard cannot change his/its spots.
(= A person cannot change his or her basic character once it has been formed.)
She's got crow's feet. (= She has wrinkles around her eyes.)
He's the black sheep of his family.
(= He's very different from the rest of his family.)
She's got ants in her pants. (= She is restless.)
He is a lounge lizard. (= He doesn't anything but idle around.)
It's like water off a duck's back. (= It doesn't have any effect.)

2. 학과전공 영문표기: Majors in English

- 건축학 architecture
- 경영학 business administration
- 광고홍보학 advertising & public relations
- 국어국문학 Korean language and literature (Korean)
- 국제경제통상학 international economics and trade
- 국제경제학 international economics
- 국제레저관광학 global leisure & tourism
- 국제무도경호학 international martial arts guard
- 국제학 international studies
- 기계공학 mechanical engineering
- 나노화학 nanochemistry
- 노어러시아학 Russian language and Russian studies
- 동북아학 Northeast Asian studies
- 디스플레이학 information display
- 문화컨텐츠학 culture & content
- 물리학 physics
- 법학 law
- 북한학 North Korea studies
- 사회복지학 social welfare
- 산업경영공학 industrial and management engineering
- 상담산업심리학 counseling and industrial psychology
- 생명화학공학 biochemical engineering
- 생물자원과학 biological resources science
- 수산생명의학 aquatic life medical science
- 수학 mathematics
- 순결학 pure love
- 스페인어중남미학 Spanish language and Latin American studies
- 스포츠과학 sports science
- 시각디자인학 visual design
- 식품과학 food science
- 신문방송학 journalism and mass communications
- 신소재공학 advanced materials engineering

- 신소재과학 advanced materials science
- IT경영학 information technology management
- 역사학 historical sciences (History)
- 영어 English
- 응용생물학 applied biology
- 의생명과학 biomedical science
- 일어일본학 Japanese language and Japanese studies (Japanese)
- 전자공학 electronic engineering
- 전자재료공학 electronic materials engineering
- 정보통신공학 information and communications engineering
- 제약공학 pharmaceutical engineering
- 제어계측공학 control and measurement engineering
- 중어중국학 Chinese language and Chinese studies (Chinese)
- 지식정보산업공학 knowledge industrial engineering
- 철학 philosophy
- 컴퓨터공학 computer engineering
- 컴퓨터정보학 computer and information science
- 토목공학 civil engineering
- 통일신학 unification theology
- 하이브리드공학 hybrid engineering
- 한국언어문화학 Korean language and culture studies
- 행정학 public administration
- 화학 chemistry
- 화학공학 chemical engineering
- 환경공학 environment engineering

3. 직업명칭 영문표기: Jobs in English

- 가수 a singer
- 가정교사 a tutor
- 가정부 a housekeeper
- 가정주부 a housewife, a homemaker
- 간호사 a nurse
- 감독 a director
- 감독관 a supervisor
- 강사 an instructor
- 건축가 an architect
- 검사 a prosecutor
- 경리 a bookkeeper
- 경비원 a security guard
- 경비직원 a security personnel
- 경영자 a manager
- 경찰관 a police officer
- 고고학자 an archaeologist
- 고문(컨설턴트) a consultant
- 곡예사 an acrobat
- 공무원 a government worker
- 공인재무관리사
  a certified financial manager
- 공인회계사 a certified public accountant
- 공장관리자 a plant manager
- 공증인 a notary public, a notary
- 과학자 a scientist
- 관리인 a manager
- 광고대행업자 a publicity agent
- 광부 a miner
- 교도관 a prison guard
- 교사 a teacher
- 교수 a professor
- 교장 a principal
- 교정원 a proofreader
- 구청직원 a ward officer
- 국무총리 the Prime Minister
- 국회의원 an Assemblyman, a Congressman
- 군인 a military personnel
- 기계공 a mechanic
- 기술자 an engineer
- 기자 a reporter
- 꽃장수 a florist
- 노동자 a laborer
- 농부 a farmer
- 뉴스앵커 an anchorperson
- 대금업자 a moneylender
- 대부업자 a moneylender
- 대서인 a scrivener
- 대통령 the President
- 도매상인 a wholesale dealer, a wholesaler
- 도서관사서 a librarian
- 도시계획자 a city planner
- 동물조련사 an animal trainer
- 매표인 a ticket agent
- 목사 a paster, a priest, a minister
- 목수 a carpenter
- 무용수 a dancer
- 문서정리원 a file clerk
- 물리학자 a physicist
- 미술가 an artist
- 미용사 a hair dresser, a beautician
- 배달원 a carrier, a delivery man
- 배우 an actor, an actress
- 버스운전사 a bus driver
- 번역가 a translator

- 법무사 a judicial scrivener
- 법무장관 the Attorney General
- 벽돌공 a bricklayer
- 변리사 a patent agent, a patent attorney
- 변호사 a lawyer, an attorney
- 보험중개인 an insurance agent
- 부동산중개인 a real estate agent, a reality dealer, a realtor
- 부서책임자 a manager
- 부통령 the Vice President
- 비밀요원 a secret agent
- 비서 a secretary
- 비행기조종사 a pilot
- 사립탐정 a private detective, a private investigator
- 사무원 a clerk
- 사장 a president
- 사진사 a photographer
- 상담원(카운셀러) a counselor
- 생물학자 a biologist
- 서류정리원 a file clerk
- 선원 a sailor, a mariner
- 선장 a captain
- 성우 a voice actor
- 성직자 a minister
- 세무사 a certified tax accountant
- 세탁업자 a laundryman
- 소매상인 a retail dealer, a retailer
- 소방수 a fire fighter
- 소설가 a novelist
- 수녀 a nun
- 수의사 a veterinarian
- 슈퍼마켓점원 a supermarket clerk
- 승무원 a flight attendant
- 시인 a poet
- 시장 a mayor
- 식료품상인 a grocer
- 신문기자 a journalist
- 심리학자 a psychologist
- 아나운서 an announcer
- 안전요원 a safety guard
- 야구선수 a baseball player
- 어부 a fisher, a fisherman
- 언론인 a journalist
- 연구원 an investigator
- 연예인 an entertainer
- 영업사원 a sales representative
- 예술가 an artist
- 예언자 a prophet
- 외교관 a diplomat
- 요리사 a cook, a chef
- 우주비행사 an astronaut
- 우체부 a mail carrier
- 운동선수 an athlete
- 웹디자이너 a web designer
- 유통관리사 a certified distribution manager
- 은행가 a banker
- 은행출납원 a teller
- 음악가 a musician
- 의사 a doctor
- 이발사 a barber
- 임시교원 a substitute teacher
- 자동차정비공 a car mechanic, an auto mechanic
- 자동차판매업자 a car dealer, an automobile dealer
- 자영업자 a self-employer
- 작가 an author, a writer
- 재봉사 a tailor, a dressmaker
- 전기공 an electrician

- 전당포업자 a pawnbroker
- 전업주부 a housewife, a homemaker
- 전화교환원 a telephone operator
- 접수계원 a receptionist
- 정육점주인 a butcher
- 정치가 a politician, a statesman
- 제빵사 a baker
- 조사관 an inspector
- 주방장 a cook, a chef
- 주식중개인 a stock broker
- 중장비기사 a heavy equipment operator
- 지배인 a manager
- 직업군인 a professional soldier
- 책편집자 a book editor
- 출납원 a cashier
- 출판업자 a publisher
- 치과의사 a dentist
- 커피재배가 a coffee grower
- 타이피스트 a typist
- 탐정 a detective, an investigator
- 탐험가 an explorer
- 택시운전사 a taxi driver
- 통역사 an interpreter
- 판매원 a salesperson
- 판사 a judge
- 패션디자이너 a fashion designer
- 편집자 an editor
- 피아니스트 a pianist
- 하수도배관공 a plumber
- 화가 a painter
- 화훼가 a florist
- 회계사 an accountant

4. 자기소개 및 가족관련 표현

1. A: Where are you from?
B: I'm from the United States.

2. A: Have you ever been to the States?
B: Once. I was there for a week.

3. A: What took you to the States?
B: I visited my grandparents in New York.

4. A: What brings you to Korea?
B: I'm here as an exchange student.

5. A: I don't think we've met.
B: My name is John Kim. Nice to meet you.

6. A: What do you do?
B: I'm a student.

7. A: Where do you live?
B: I live in Asan.

8. A: Do you live in a house or an apartment?
B: I live in an apartment.

9. A: Are you from around here?
B: Yes, I live near here.

10. A: Can I get you something to drink?
B: Yes, thank you. A Coke, please.

11. A: How do you know John?
B: We're classmates. We're in the same English class.

12. A: What's your name?
B: My name is Emily Kwon.

12. A: What do people call you?
B: Please call me Emily. (= Everybody calls me Emily.)

13. A: What's your last name again?
B: It's Kwon.

14. A: How do you spell your last name?
B: K-W-O-N.

15. A: How many people are there in your family?
B: There are six in my family.

16. A: How many brothers and sisters do you have?
B: I have two sisters and a brother.

17. A: Tell me about your family.
B: There are three of us. I'm an only child.

18. A: How big is your family?
B: I have a family of four. My parents, my younger sister, and I.

18. A: Do you live with your family?
B: No, I live alone in Cheonan.

19. A: What is he like?
B: He's very smart and funny.

20. A: What does she look like?
B: She's very tall and beautiful.

21. A: Who's that?
B: She's my sister.

22. A: Your sister is so cute. How old is she?
B: She's 16 years old.

23. A: How old are your parents?
B: My father is 47 years old and my mother is 46 years old.

24. A: What do your parents do?
B: My father is an architecture and my mother is a housewife.

25. A: Does your father like his job?
B: Yes, he loves it.

26. A: What's his job like?
B: It's very exciting but difficult.

27. A: What are you going to do this weekend?
B: I'm afraid I need to stay home all weekend.
I have a lot of homework to do.

28. A: Are you coming to our club field trip this Saturday?
B: Please count me out. I'm afraid I won't be able to make it this time.
My grandmother is coming to Korea on Saturday, so I need to meet her at the airport.

29. A: I'm looking for a one-bedroom apartment now.
B: If you're interested, I think there is an empty apartment in my building.

30. A: Why don't you come look at my place this evening? If you like it, we can ask the rental office about the empty one.
B: OK. That sounds like a good idea. Thanks.

5. 음식 및 식당주문관련 영어표현

1. A: Do you want to go out for dinner tonight?
B: Sure. Where would you like to go?

2. A: What's your favorite food?
B: I really like pizza.

3. A: What kind of food do you like best?
B: I love Chinese food.

4. A: I'm crazy about Chinese food.
B: So am I. (= I am, too.)

5. A: I like Japanese food a lot.
B: So do I. (= I do, too.)

6. A: I can't stand greasy food.
B: Neither can I. (= I can't, either. = Me, neither.)

7. A: I don't like salty food.
B: Oh, I like it a lot.

8. A: Do you like Kal-gook-soo?
B: No, I can't eat bland food.

9. A: Who do you have lunch with?
B: I have lunch with my club members.

10. A: It's raining outside. Let's have lunch delivered here.
B: OK. Let's order in some Chinese food.

11. A: I'm in the mood for something delicious tonight.
B: Hey, why don't we have some pizza delivered.

12. A: What do you want to have for dinner?
B: I'm in the mood for something spicy.

13. A: Let's eat out tonight.
B: OK. That sounds like a good idea.

14. A: What would you like to order, sir?
B: I'll have the fish cutlet.

15. A: May I take your order?
B: I'd like a steak.

16. A: How would you like your steak?
B: Medium-rare, please.

17. A: Would you like to have cream soup or vegetable soup?
B: I'll have cream soup, please.

18. A: Would you like rice or potatoes?
B: Potatoes, please.

19. A: What kind of potatoes would you like?
Mashed, baked, or french fries?
B: I'd like baked potatoes.

20. A: What will you have to drink?
B: I'll have a cup of coffee.

21. A: Would you like dessert? We have cake, pie, and ice cream.
B: Yes, I'd like ice cream.

22. A: What flavor would you like? We have vanilla, strawberry, and chocolate.
B: I'll have chocolate ice cream, please.

23. A: What kind of pie do you have?
B: We have apple and cherry.

24. A: Excuse me, we didn't order this wine.
B: Don't worry. This is on the house. Happy birthday!

24. A: I'll pick up the tab. This is my treat.
B: No way! Your money is no good today. It's on me.

25. A: Let's go Dutch.
B: OK. Let's split it.

6. 성격관련 영어표현-형용사형

1. He's very outgoing. 그는 활달하고 외향적이다. (= He's extroverted.)
2. He's reserved. 그는 내성적이다. (= He's introverted.)
3. He's smart and funny. 그는 똑똑하고 사람을 잘 웃긴다.
4. He's good-hearted. 그는 참 착하다.
5. He's friendly. 그는 상냥하고 친절하다.
6. He's naive. 그는 순진하다.
7. He's active. 그는 적극적이다.
8. He's shy. 그는 수줍음이 많다. / 그는 소극적이다.
9. He's quiet. 그는 조용하다.
10. He's talkative. 그는 말이 많다.
11. He's generous. 그는 관대하다.
12. He's mean. 그는 야비하다.
13. He's optimistic. 그는 낙천적/낙관적이다.
14. He's pessimistic. 그는 폐쇄적/염세적이다.
15. He's sensitive. 그는 섬세/예민하다.
16. He's insensitive. 그는 둔감하다.
17. He's ambitious. 그는 의욕적이다.
18. He's reliable. 그는 믿을만한 사람이다.
19. He's serious. 그는 매사에 진지하다.
20. He's very punctual. 그는 시간을 참 잘 지킨다.
21. He's always late. 그는 항상 지각한다.
22. He's hard-working. 그는 부지런하다.
23. He's lazy. 그는 게으르다.
24. He's easy-going. 그는 느긋한 형이다.
25. He's honest. 그는 정직하다.
26. He's dishonest. 그는 부정직하다.
27. He's flexible. 그는 융통성이 있다.

28. He's inflexible. 그는 융통성이 없다. / 그는 완고하다.
29. He's modest. 그는 겸손하다.
30. He's selfish. 그는 이기적이다.
31. He's sincere. 그는 성실하다.
32. He's rude. 그는 무례하다.
33. He's impolite. 그는 예의가 없다.
34. He's mischievous. 근 장난기가 심하다. / 그는 심술궂다
35. He's arrogant. 그는 거만하다.
36. He's very cheerful. 그는 매우 밝고 명랑하다.
37. He's sociable. 그는 사교적이다.
38. He's fickle. 그는 변덕스럽다.
39. He's short-tempered. 그는 성격이 급하다.
40. He's very forgetful. 그는 건망증이 심하다.
41. He's thoughtful. 그는 사려 깊다.
42. He's open-minded. 그는 포용력이 있다.
43. He's wishy-washy. 그는 술에 술탄 듯 물에 물탄 듯하다. / 그는 우유부단하다.
44. He's clever. 그는 영리하다.
45. He's creative. 그는 창의력이 있다.
46. He's sympathetic. 그는 동정심이 있다.
47. He's stingy. 그는 인색하다.
48. He's conservative. 그는 보수적이다.
49. He's strict. 그는 엄격하다.
50. He's good-natured. 그는 본성이 착하다.

7. 성향관련 영어표현-명사형

1. She's a dollar-watcher. 그녀는 검약가다. / 그녀는 검소한 사람이다.
2. She's a penny-pincher. 그녀는 구두쇠다. (= She's a cheapskate.)
3. She's a money grabber. 그녀는 돈이라면 사족을 못 쓰는 사람이다.
4. She's a deadbeat. 그녀는 절대로 돈을 갚지 않는 사람이다. / 그녀는 돈을 떼어먹는 사람이다.
5. She's a free-loader. 그녀는 공짜로 얻어먹기를 좋아하는 사람이다. / 그녀는 빈대다.
6. She's a good singer. 그녀는 노래를 참 잘한다.
7. She's a computer whiz. 그녀는 컴퓨터 도사다.
8. She's a mouse potato. 그녀는 컴퓨터광이다.
9. She's a video game buff. 그녀는 비디오게임광이다.
10. She's a speed buff. 그녀는 속도광이다.
11. She's a junk food junkie. 그녀는 패스트푸드광이다.
12. She's a sports fan. 그녀는 스포츠광이다.
13. She's a clean bug. 그녀는 결벽주의자다. (= She's a neat freak.)
14. She's a cleaning bug. 그녀는 청소하기를 좋아한다.
15. She's a litterbug. 그녀는 쓰레기를 아무데나 버리는 사람이다.
16. She's butterfingers. 그녀는 물건을 잘 떨어뜨린다. (= She has butterfingers.)
17. She's an ice breaker. 그녀는 분위기 메이커이다.
18. She's the life of the party. 그녀는 분위기 메이커이다.
19. She's a wet blanket. 그녀는 분위기 망치는 사람이다. / 그녀는 흥을 깨는 사람이다.
20. She's a party pooper. 그녀는 분위기 망치는 사람이다. / 그녀는 흥을 깨는 사람이다.
21. She's a spoil sport. 그녀는 분위기 망치는 사람이다. / 그녀는 흥을 깨는 사람이다.
22. She's a pain in the neck. 그녀는 골치 덩어리다. (= She's a pain in the side.)
23. She's a good gardener. 그녀는 원예솜씨가 있다. (= She has a green thumb.)
24. She's not a good gardener. 그녀는 원예솜씨가 없다. (= She has a brown thumb.)
25. She's a heavy sleeper. 그녀는 잠귀가 어둡다. / 그녀는 한번 자면 업어 가도 모른다.
26. She's a light sleeper. 그녀는 잠귀가 밝다. / 그녀는 잠을 깊게 자지 못하는 사람이다.
27. She's a cold fish. 그녀는 냉정한 사람이다.

28. She's a big mouth. 그녀는 허풍쟁이다. (= She's a loud mouth.)
29. She's a smooth talker. 그녀는 말을 잘한다.
30. She's got a silver tongue. 그녀는 능변가다.
31. She's a soft-spoken person. 그녀는 말을 부드럽게 한다.
32. She's a self-made woman. 그녀는 자수성가한 사람이다.
33. She's a five-finger discounter. 그녀는 도벽이 있다. (= She has sticky fingers.)
34. She's number one. 그녀는 훌륭한 사람이다. (= She's something/somebody.)
35. She's number ten. 그녀는 형편없는 사람이다.(= She's nothing/nobody.)
36. She is a light eater.그녀는 소식가예요. (= She eats like a bird.)
37. She's a picky eater. (= She's picky/particular/choosy about food.)
38. She's a double-crosser. 그녀는 배신자다.
39. She's a two-timer. 그녀는 양다리 걸치는 사람이에요. / 그녀는 바람둥이에요.
40. She's a serial dater. 그녀는 연애꾼이다. / 그녀는 애인을 너무 자주 바꾸는 사람이다.
41. She's a budget traveler. 그녀는 알뜰여행자이다.
42. She's a budget shopper. 그녀는 알뜰쇼핑객이다.
43. She's a stiff-arm driver. 그녀는 팔에 잔뜩 힘을 주고 운전하는 사람이다.
44. She's a shopaholic. 그녀는 쇼핑중독자이다. (= She's a shopping addict.)
45. She's a workaholic. 그녀는 일중독자/일벌레다.
46. She's a chocoholic. 그녀는 초콜릿 중독자다.
47. She's a bookworm. 그녀는 독서광/책벌레이다.
48. She's an overpacker. 그녀는 여행 가방을 크게 싸는 사람이다.
49. She's a road hog. 그녀는 도로를 혼자 독차지하고 난폭하게 운전하는 사람이다.
50. She's a do-it-yourselfer. 그녀는 무슨 일이든지 직접 하기를 좋아하는 사람이다.
(= She's a do-it-yourself fan.)

8. 질병관련 영어표현

1. I have a headache. 나는 머리가 아프다.
2. I have a migraine headache. 나는 편두통이 있다.
3. I have an earache. 나는 귀가 아프다.
4. I have a toothache. 나는 치통이 있다.
5. I have buck teeth. 나는 뻐드렁니가 있다.
6. I have wisdom teeth. 나는 사랑니가 있다.
7. I have a stomachache. 나는 배가 아프다.
8. I have stomach cramps. 나는 위경련이 있다. / 나는 배가 부글부글 끓는다.
9. I have a backache. 나는 등이 아프다.
10. I have a sore throat. 나는 목구멍이 아프다.
11. I have a stiff neck. 나는 목이 뻐근하다.
12. I have sore eyes. 나는 눈이 아프다.
13. I have pinkeye. 나는 눈병이 났다.
14. I have a cold. 나는 감기에 걸렸다. (= I caught cold)
15. I have a head cold, 나는 코감기에 걸렸다.
16. I have a runny nose. 나는 콧물이 난다. (= My nose is runny.)
17. I have a bloody nose. 나는 코피가 난다.
18. I have a stuffy nose. 나는 코가 막혀서 답답하다.
19. I have the flu. 나는 독감에 걸렸다.
20. I have a sneeze. 나는 재채기가 난다.
21. I have a cough. 나는 기침이 난다.
22. I have sore muscles. 나는 근육통이 있다. (= I have a muscle pain)
23. I have a burn. 나는 화상을 입었다.
24. I have a fever. 나는 열이 있다. (= I have a temperature.)
25. I have a stiff shoulder. 어깨가 뻐근하다.
26. I have frozen shoulder. 나는 오십견이 있다.
27. I have swimmer's shoulder. 나는 어깨가 아프다. / 나는 어깨 관절이 아프다.

28. I have loose bowels. 나는 설사를 한다. (= I have diarrhea. / I have the runs)

29. I have constipation 나는 변비가 있다.

30. I have piles. 나는 치질로 고생한다. (= I have hemorhoids.)

31. I have insomnia. 나는 불면증으로 고생한다.

32. I have a rash. 나는 발진이 난다.

33. I have a blister. 나는 물집이 생겼다.

34. I have a boil. 나는 종기가 났다.

35. I have sore fingers. 나는 손가락이 아프다.

36. I have athlete's foot. 나는 무좀이 있다.

37. I have football knee. 나는 무릎관절이 아프다.

38. I have an insect bite. 나는 벌레한테 물렸다.

39. I have morning sickness. 나는 입덧을 한다.

40. I have the hiccups. 나는 딸꾹질을 한다.

41. I have bad breath. 나는 입냄새가 난다.

42. I have food poisoning. 나는 식중독이다.

43. I have a herniated disk. 나는 허리디스크를 앓고 있다.

44. I have arthritis. 나는 관절염이 있다.

45. I have diabetes. 나는 당뇨병이 있다.

46. I have osteoporosis. 나는 골다공증이 있다.

47. I have tonsillitis. 나는 편도선염이 있다.

48. I have anemia. 나는 빈혈이 있다.

49. I have leukemia. 나는 백혈병에 걸려 있다.

50. I have high blood pressure. 나는 고혈압이 있다. (= I have hypertension.)

Situational English

2009년 02월 19재판
2009년 02월 20발행

저 자 김 선 옥
발행인 김 봉 태
발행처 선문대학교 출판부
336-708 충청남도 아산시 탕정면 갈산리 100
전화 (041)530-2114 / Fax. (041)530-2979
등록 제9호
정가 8,000원
ISBN 978-89-8423-636-3 12740